electronic music circuit guidebook

Other TAB books by Brice Ward

No. 743
$9.95

electronic music circuit guidebook

by brice ward

TAB BOOKS
Blue Ridge Summit, Pa. 17214

Preface

There are books on organ repair, construction, and design; there are books on electronic equipment used to amplify, distort, reverberate, and otherwise change the quality of sound from some musical instrument. Occasionally these will contain references to music synthesizers and similar exotic circuitry. Some even have a few photographs of the Moog or some other synthesizer.

Few of these books, however, contain the actual circuits used in these mysterious and exotic instruments. And although the list of circuits that *could* be used is endless, there are *few* of these that can, when properly patched together, generate a veritable infinity of unusual music and sound effects.

It is this kind of electronic music this book is about. You will find circuits for percussion generators, voltage-controlled oscillators, ring modulators, envelope shapers, and a number of other peripheral items.

Obtaining this material has been no easy task. Each circuit, each bit of information, and each new idea has been carefully assimilated, recorded, and hoarded for the sole purpose of one day writing a book to save others the problems I have had in finding the information.

To me, there is nothing more satisfying than to make sounds of any type come from a speaker; and if you share this interest, this book is for you.

This book would not have been as long nor as useful without the help of PAIA Electronics, Inc. PAIA has allowed me to borrow extensively from the material supplied with their **Gnome** and 2700 series music synthesizer kits, whose circuits were designed by John S. Simonton, Jr., president of PAIA Electronics. The circuits can be built in all cases by the serious experimenter, or kits can be obtained in many instances from the manufacturer: PAIA Electronics, Inc., Box 14359, Oklahoma City 73114.

Brice Ward

Contents

1 | An Introduction to Electronic Sound

There are really only three characteristics that determine what a musical instrument will sound like: pitch, dynamics, and timbre. Of the three, pitch probably requires the least explanation.

Pitch and frequency are two words from two different technologies that describe the same thing. When an engineer or technician speaks of 261 Hz, he means that the thing they are referring to is vibrating 261 times per second. When a musician mentions middle C he is also talking about something that is vibrating 261 times per second. If the musician is dealing with conventional instruments he is probably talking about a string or reed, but if he is working with an organ or synthesizer he is likely referring to the same thing that the technologists were talking about, the frequency of the changes of an electrical waveform.

SOUND AS AN ELECTRICAL ANALOG

The human ear is more sensitive to changes in pitch than any other musical parameter. The intensity of a sound has to be cut significantly before a listener experiences any decrease is loudness, but a skilled musician can tell when a musical semitone deviates by as little as 3% of the interval between that note and the next higher tone.

Dynamics is a broad term that refers to the time-varying intensity characteristics of the sound—how fast it builds up and how fast it dies away.

The length of time required for a sound to build up to its greatest intensity is called *attack time*, and this one parameter conveys more information about the way an instrument is played than any other. If the attack time is very short the instrument will be in the percussion family where the vibrating member is immediately excited to its maximum amplitude by the deforming action of being plucked or struck with a hammer or mallet. If the attack is relatively slow then the instrument is probably in the reed or bowed-string groups where the action of the exciting force—the wind or bow of the performer—takes a short time to fully excite the vibrating element.

If you forget about the talent factor for a moment, the primary purpose of the musician in playing most instruments is to serve as an energy source. The performer pumps energy into the system (instrument) and the system dissipates it in some way, usually either as sound or heat. If you were able to accurately measure the temperature of a drum head you'd find that it gets hotter as you pound on it. The energy that is converted to heat can be thought of as being lost since it does not contribute to the primary object of producing sound. And so another important characteristic of an instrument is its *decay time*—that is, how fast the sound dies away. Decay time is directly related to how much of the energy goes into heat and how much into sound. A vibrating string, for instance, is as close to lossless as you can get and its decay time is very long. The stretched membrance of a drumhead on the other hand is very lossy and as a result the decay time of drums is very short.

Reed instruments have a short decay time because the reeds are relatively lossy and don't continue to vibrate for very long after the musician stops adding energy. Brass instruments have the shortest decay time because the performer can force his lips to stop vibrating and the column of air in the instrument is very lossy.

Sustain time is the interval between attack and decay, the steady-state response of the instrument. As is obvious, percussion instruments have zero sustain time; as soon as the attack is finished there is no more energy input so it's downhill the rest of the way. Instruments that have some continuous energy input from the performer, in the form of bowing, blowing or even pedaling in the case of some organs, can sustain as long as the energy holds out.

Though attack, sustain, and decay are the primary phenomena of dynamics there is one other condition that is common enough to merit a separate section. When a percussion instrument is struck very hard the vibrating member will deform beyond the point at which a smooth decay is possible; in effect, more energy is put into the system than it can handle, with a resulting overload. Under these conditions the system (string, membrane, or whatever) will rapidly get rid of the excess energy. With the overload dissipated, the vibrating element will continue to dissipate the remaining energy in a normal fashion. The result is an initial rapid attack immediately followed by a *release time*, which is then followed by a normal decay. In a natural instrument it would be all but impossible for the release time to be followed by a sustain interval, but with a synthesizer this is simple.

We can graphically illustrate the conditions discussed by plotting the *overall intensity* of the sound versus time as shown in Fig. 1-1. Since these graphs are drawn to show the peak amplitude of the sound at any given time and therefore "contain" the sound, they are often referred to as envelopes.

It is pretty obvious that as important as dynamics might be, it doesn't account for all the differences between the sounds of instruments. For instance, the trumpet and French horn are both brass instruments with approximately the same attack, sustain, and decay characteristics. They even overlap as far as pitch range is concerned; but there would be little danger of mistaking the blaring, brassy sound of the trumpet for the mellow, muted tones of the French horn. These differences come about because no musical instrument produces a tone that is composed exclusively of a single frequency. Each note is composed of a number of different frequencies, and the number and amplitude of the various components are what gives each instrument its distinctive *timbre*.

Harmonics

The concept that a single musical pitch can be made up of more than one frequency can be confusing and needs further attention. The sine wave is the basic building block of any imaginable accoustic or electrical wave. It is the only waveform that is composed entirely of a single frequency and,

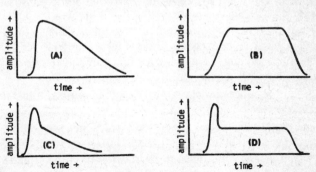

Fig. 1-1. Amplitude envelopes for (A) percussion, (B) reeds, (C) attack-release-decay, (D) attack-release-sustain-decay.

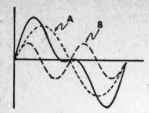

Fig. 1-2. Fundamental and second harmonic.

more importantly, any waveform can be built up using nothing but sine waves.

Look at Fig. 1-2. Here we have two sine waves drawn in dotted lines which are labeled *A* and *B*; as you can see from the drawing, waveform *B* goes through two cycles in the time that it takes waveform *A* to complete a single cycle. Waveform *B* is therefore twice the frequency of *A* and is said to be the second harmonic of the *fundamental frequency* A. If we draw another wave that is three times the frequency of *A* it would be the third harmonic, four times would be the fourth harmonic, five times the fifth, and so on.

If at every point in time we sum together the amplitudes of waveforms *A* and *B*, the result is the waveform shown by the solid line. Note that while the new wave is shaped differently than either *A* or *B* it has the same frequency (and consequently pitch) as the fundamental frequency *A*. If third, fourth, fifth and higher order harmonics were added into this wave the result would continue to change shape but the frequency would remain the same.

It is not necessary that *every* harmonic of a fundamental frequency be included in a wave and indeed the most musically interesting sounds have certain harmonics deleted. The square wave is a good example. It is difficult to imagine that the sharp-edged square wave could be built up from smoothly changing sine waves, but it can be, as shown in Fig. 1-3. In sketch A, a fundamental frequency is added to its third harmonic, producing the waveform shown by the solid line. In sketch B the fifth harmonic has been added to the result of sketch A to produce the new solid waveform; in sketch C the seventh harmonic has been added to all the rest. You can see that the trend as higher order harmonics are added is to steepen the sides of the square and flatten and reduce the ripple in the top. When enough harmonics have been added, the result will be a square wave. Notice in particular that not all harmonics are added together for a square wave, only the *odd* harmonics are included.

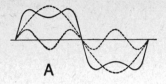

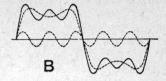

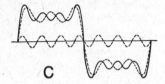

Fig.1-3. Square wave composition.

The keyboard, with contacts brought out conveniently, will also prove very useful. It *is* possible to use pushbutton switches and similar gadgets for keying oscillators, but the satisfaction of a keyboard and its capability as a real musical-instrument component make it a near necessity for a studio.

Pitch

Amplifiers are designed to work from 20 Hz to 20 kHz. It is my personal contention that the range should be broadened to include those frequencies between DC and 100 kHz. The human ear is able to hear sine waves to around 15 kHz at the upper extreme and not much below 40 Hz at the lower. But the overtones and undertones (harmonics and subharmonics) and the attack and decay characteristics of instruments, voice, and other sound sources are sensed as *elements* of sounds within the audible spectrum. However, I will limit the discussion to frequencies below 20,000 Hz, since that is a widely accepted figure for the limit of human hearing.

The 9-octave range of an electronic organ covers frequencies from 16 to 7900 Hz. There will be harmonics far above the last figure in a square wave of 7900 Hz, but although we will be interested in reproducing these frequencies, we will confine ourselves to generating only those 9 octaves.

But here is the essential first ingredient for the development of a sound. Some fundamental frequency between 16 and 8000 Hz must be generated. Overtones can be developed at the same time, or they could be mixed later or created artificially by reshaping the fundamental frequency.

Now, although we will present devices for generating frequencies across this entire spectrum in a continuous mode, we will also present both linear and digital circuitry for generating discrete sine, square, and triangular waves in a chromatic scale.

Intensity

The intensity or loudness of a sound is measured in decibels. This might be considered the second most important characteristic of any sound generated. The upper figure of 180 dB is some 60 dB above the "threshold of painful sound" at about 120 dB.

A quiet whisper at 5 feet reaches a level of 18 dB while an express subway will reach something on the order of 100 dB. Although interesting, these figures do not have a great deal of bearing on music, except as it relates to the total dynamic range of the human ear.

Envelope

The real beginning of character for musical sound begins with the shaping of intensity versus time. Figure 1-4 shows the characteristics of major interest. These are *attack* (actually, the rise time to some relatively steady level of intensity), *sustain* or steady-state character, and *decay*. The entire sequence, which may be far more complex than is shown, will have some specific *duration*.

Taking a few examples, a bowed instrument such as a violin will have a relatively slow *attack*. The *sustain* will be determined by the violinist, and the *decay* will be relatively quick. A piano string, on the other hand, is struck by a hammer. The result is a very quick *attack*, followed by an

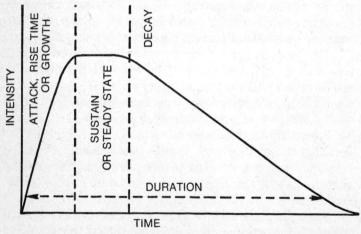

Fig. 1-4. Attack-sustain-decay waveform.

immediate *decay*—which may be either fast or slow, depending on the *sustain* pedal that controls damping.

These two instruments, even though both are string instruments, will have *very* different sound characteristics, determined largely by the shape of the intensity-versus-time envelope. For this reason, envelope shaping circuits will be given considerable treatment later.

Timbre

There are at least five other characteristics that occur naturally or can be introduced artificially to contribute to the character of a sound. The first of these is *timbre*, which denotes the characteristic imparted to a sound by a number of other frequencies mixed in varying proportion to the fundamental or basic frequency. These may or may not be harmonics of the fundamental. A carillon is not a very "harmonious" bell, but its sound is certainly not unpleasant.

Timbre is put into a piano note by the introduction of more than one string, where each string is tuned differently. In the electronic or pipe organ timbre is effected by mixing, via the *stops*, various combinations of frequencies from oscillators, dividers, or other sources. The resulting sounds are given names, some of which relate to instruments they simulate (flute) or to completely new sounds (diapason).

The second characteristic is *glide* or *portamento*. When the frequency of a note changes during the playing to another note in a continuous manner, actually running through all intermediate frequencies, the resulting sound is a glide. The Hawaiian steel guitar is perhaps the best example of an instrument that makes extensive use of this characteristic.

Vibrato and *tremolo* are two separate effects that are frequently confused. Vibrato is the low-frequency variation of the basic frequency of a sound around some center frequency. The depth of vibrato is the total frequency deviation caused by the vibrato signal; the frequency of this deviation is usually around 7 Hz, although other frequencies could certainly be used.

Tremolo, on the other hand, normally refers to a similar variation of the intensity or amplitude of a sound. The basic frequency used to achieve the effect is the same (7 Hz) and the two effects are similar enough in final result to be easily confused.

Finally, a rather vague thing called deviation, which could affect frequency, intensity, envelope shaping, or any other characteristic is introduced as a catchall. We will deal with circuits to produce deviation, but they will be called reverb units, ring modulators, and other things.

SOUND SOURCES

Probably the first sound sources that come to mind are the human voice and various musical instruments. Leaving the human voice for a minute, instruments are categorized into four major classes based largely on the type of medium or device used to produce the basic pitch. The class known as *strings*, for example, includes those instruments which use mechanical strings that produce sounds by vibration in a complex mode. Further character will be imparted by the system used to set the strings in motion. In this way a plucked string, a bowed string, and a hammered string each have a different sound characteristic.

Woodwinds have a sound developed by the vibration of a bamboo or plastic reed against a mouthpiece (single-reed) or against another reed (double-reed). The saxophone and clarinet fall in the first category, and oboe and bassoon fall in the second.

Brass instruments have a mouthpiece that makes use of lip vibrations to produce the sound. The shape and length of the horn produce various pitches and timbres for such instruments. These are represented by the trumpet, French horn, tuba, and similar instruments.

The *percussion* instruments normally produce sounds around some particular basic frequency. Bass and snare drums, cymbals, gongs, triangles, and so forth fall in the percussion category—The chief difference is their respective characteristic frequencies. The piano is a combination of percussion and string. The string predominates because there is a good deal of fundamental sine-wave content. Cymbals, on the other hand, can be simulated electronically by feeding white noise through an envelope shaper.

The flute and the pipes of an organ operate on a whistle principle, while the harmonica and accordian make use of metal reeds that vibrate in an air stream.

But notice one thing. In all of these sources of sound, waves of a few or many frequencies are combined to produce the sound. Even white noise is composed of a very wide band of individual waves that can be filtered out one by one to leave nothing. After this mixture of basic frequencies, which comprise pitch and timbre, there is a variation of intensity or loudness. This is the final and very important part of any instrumental sound. Other small deviations can be introduced, but most of the sounds of various instruments can be electronically produced by mixing the proper frequencies and putting them through an *envelope shaper*.

The envelope shaper and other sound treatments will be considered in more detail under that heading. Here we will continue to concern ourselves with sound sources of an electronic nature. This means, basically, oscillators of one sort or another.

We could, and will, start with simple oscillators as sound sources and develop a number of concepts from here. To begin with, *something* must vibrate or oscillate to produce pitch. But how many are required? What type should they be? Should they run continuously or be keyed? Should they be tunable and, if so, to what frequency? And to all of these questions there is only one answer: It depends entirely on what you want to achieve!

One thing *can* be said about *any* such oscillator. It *must be stable*. If it is a fixed pitch tunable oscillator for an organ or similar instrument, once tuned it should remain very accurately on frequency for long periods. If it is a VCO (voltage-controlled oscillator), it should not only hold its pitch when a control voltage is applied but this precise pitch for a given voltage should be repeatable. And at this point it would be well to consider the chromatic scale and see not only what a scale is but what types of errors can be detected by the human ear.

An octave in standard musical notation is 12 notes. There are 7 notes given the designations C, D, E, F, G, A, B and an additional 5 given #(sharp) designations ($C^\#$, $D^\#$, $F^\#$, $G^\#$, and $A^\#$). And for those who remember *do, re, me, fa, sol, la, ti*—these correspond to C, D, E, F, G, A and B. For those who may ask where the flats went, look for a minute at Table 1-1.

A flatted note is a note just below another in pitch. A-flat will be the note just below A in pitch, or G-sharp. E-flat is, then, D-sharp and so forth. Now, with all the external appearance of being equally spaced when listened to, *do, re* and so forth are *not* equally spaced. The spaces between the 12 notes of the scale are based on the 12th root of 2 ($\sqrt[12]{2}$). My calculator tells me that the 12th root of 2 is 1.059 463 094, and if I multiply 16.351 Hz (low C) by that number, I get 17.324 (C-sharp). If I now multiply 17.324 by that number I get 18.354

Table 1-1. Equally Tempered Chromatic Scale Frequencies (in Hertz).

C	16.352	32.703	65.406	130.81	261.63	523.25	1046.50	2093.00	4186.01
C#	17.324	34.648	69.295	138.59	277.18	554.37	1108.73	2217.46	4434.92
D	18.354	36.708	73.416	146.83	293.66	587.33	1174.66	2349.32	4698.64
D#	19.445	38.890	77.781	155.56	311.13	622.25	1244.51	2489.02	4978.03
E	20.601	41.203	82.406	164.81	329.63	659.26	1318.51	2637.02	5274.04
F	21.826	43.653	87.307	174.61	349.23	698.46	1396.91	2793.83	5587.66
F#	23.124	46.249	92.499	184.99	369.99	739.99	1479.98	2959.96	5919.92
G	24.499	48.999	97.998	195.99	391.99	783.99	1567.98	3135.97	6271.93
G#	25.956	51.913	103.82	207.65	415.31	830.61	1661.22	3322.44	6644.88
A	27.500	55.000	110.00	220.00	440.00	880.00	1760.00	3520.00	7040.00
A#	29.135	58.270	116.54	233.08	466.16	932.32	1864.66	3729.31	7458.63
B	30.867	61.735	123.47	246.94	493.88	987.77	1975.53	3951.07	7902.13

and so on through the list. This is the *equally tempered scale* (ETS).

It has been experimented with and is now being experimented with but it is still in common use and is tuned usually from $A4$ (A above middle C) which is 440.0 Hz.

The $\sqrt[12]{2}$ also gives an equal percentage frequency difference between notes on the scale—this amounts to about 6%.

This 6% difference between notes (between C and $C^{\#}$ for example) is called a *semitone*; musicians call one hundredth of that interval a *cent*, making a one-cent accuracy equal to 0.06%. And we *are* coming to a point. The very best musicians can sometimes hear a 3-cent error in pitch. Put another way, a 0.18% error in pitch might be detected by someone with "perfect pitch."

Taking 440.0 Hz as a logical example, it can vary from 439.21 to 440.79 Hz without the discrepancy being detected. However, it is being played with another note that is not of that precise frequency, an unpleasant beat could be developed with even *this* small amount of drift. Here's the point: The accuracy, stability, and repeatability of a sound source must be *very* good to be useful in serious music-making.

But let's take a look at some of the possibilities. Figure 1-5 shows the basic block diagram for a sine-wave oscillator. The first inverting amplifier gives a phase shift of 180°, the second another 180°, putting the output back in phase (360°) with the input. In this way, positive feedback can be supplied to the amplifier input via a frequency-determining network.

In other types of circuits, such as a phase-shift oscillator, the generated signal is inverted at the output over the input and the frequency-determining phase-shift network supplies an additional 180° phase shift to supply positive feedback to the input to sustain oscillations.

In this type of circuit, the phase-shift feedback system is not desirable and it requires more mathematics to determine resonant frequency than does either the Wien bridge or twin-tee oscillator. Any one of these oscillators, at audio frequencies, must be controlled or varied through changes in resistance, since the required capacitors are too large to be made variable.

For a broad control of frequency range, the phase-shift and Wien bridge systems require the variation of two resistors; the twin-tee requires the variation of three resistors.

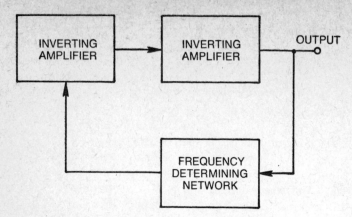

Fig. 1-5. Inversion and feedback.

Obviously, none of these circuits is really suited to voltage control, although the resistors could be made cadmium sulfide cells and their value changed by the variation of light from a light-emitting diode or a similarly fast-responding light source.

Using the resonance formula shown for the Wien bridge and twin-tee circuits (Figs. 1-6 and 1-7) and a capacitance of 0.01 μF, the resistance is 60,863Ω to generate a frequency of 261.63 Hz. The remaining values of resistance can be determined by dividing *this* value of resistance by each of the values shown in Table 1-2. The resulting resistance values are given in the table.

Several things are obvious from this. First, it is possible to calculate the required resistance values for

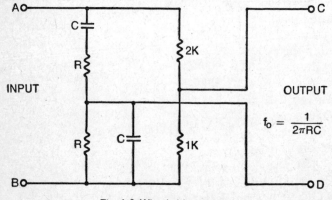

Fig. 1-6. Wien bridge network.

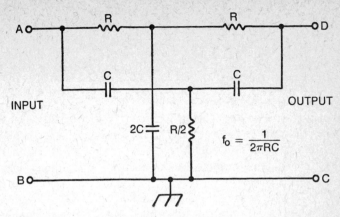

Fig. 1-7. Twin-tee network.

equally-tempered-scale (ETS) oscillators using one value of resistance calculated from a resonance formula and the remaining values using the ratios shown. Second, it is obvious that the resistance halves each octave. For 9 octaves, starting with 1 megohm (1M), we would have 500K, 250K, 125K, 62K, 31K, 16K, 8K, 4K, and 2K. It would be possible to swing through 9 octaves with one capacitor value and a 1M potentiometer, but the high frequencies would be very difficult to set because of rotation "cramping."

The ideal solution, particularly where it may be desirable to have one oscillator per note, would be to use 3 values of

Table 1-2. Derivation of Resistances for Specific Frequencies.

Note	Divisor	Resistance, K	Frequency, Hz
C	1.999999993	30.431	523.25
B	1.887748619	32.241	493.88
A#	1.781797431	34.158	466.16
A	1.681792826	36.189	440.00
G#	1.587401048	38.341	415.31
G	1.498307074	40.621	391.99
F#	1.414213560	43.037	369.99
F	1.334839852	45.596	349.23
E	1.259921048	48.307	329.63
D#	1.189207114	51.179	311.13
D	1.122462048	54.223	293.66
C#	1.059463094	57.447	277.18
C	1.000000000	60.863	261.63

capacitor (each value to cover 3 octaves) and a single-value trimmer resistor. In this way 108 oscillators would cover the full range, and each could be quite easily tuned; but sine-wave oscillators are not frequently used in either organs or synthesizers, since the waveshape doesn't match real-life instruments; so we will move on to other circuits shortly.

Sine waves are useful in demonstrating methods of achieving various frequencies for music. The important thing to understand is that the circuits do not lend themselves to low cost voltage control nor do they generate a sufficient number of harmonics to allow their use in the specialized applications of electronic music.

The nomograph of Fig. 1-8 will be useful for obtaining resistance and capacitance values for the oscillators discussed so far—it solves mechanically the formula $f_o = 1/(2\pi RC)$. Table 1-2 is a generally useful table. Each factor (from bottom to top) is the previous factor multiplied by the $\sqrt[12]{2}$ or 1.059463094. This is accurate to 9 places after the decimal point but is sufficiently inaccurate to throw the upper value, which should be 2.00, out 7 parts in the ninth decimal, so it should only be used for one octave at a time, allowing the frequency of 100 Hz, 220 Hz, 440 Hz and so forth to be the guiding figure. The resistance values and frequencies listed in Table 1-2 have already been explained.

We have been discussing one type of sound source, the sine-wave oscillator. In addition to that and *white* and *pink* noise, we will need square waves, triangular waves, and ramps—these will be used both as primary sound sources and as control voltages for voltage-controlled oscillators (vcos). It is, for example, possible to mix a fast ramp with a slower ramp and obtain a step voltage which can, in turn, be applied to a vco at audio frequencies to obtain a musical scale.

If the output of an oscillator is applied to a reverberator, the output of the reverberator can be considered a new sound source. Likewise, a tape recording can be a sound source. For this reason it is recommended that a fairly good quality tape recorder with separate dual record and playback heads be obtained for serious work with music synthesis. In this way one part of a composition can be played and recorded, then the second part or several additional parts can be played and added to what has already been done to make very complex recordings.

Perhaps one of the most unusual sounds you can obtain (for sheer novelty) is a recording of a piano with the recording

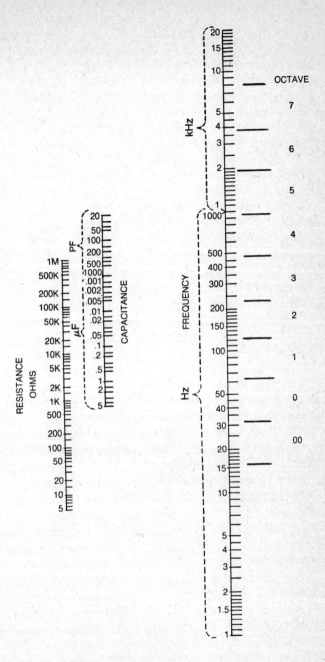

Fig. 1-8. Nomograph for R, C, and f values.

Table 1-3. Frequency Division for Note Generation.

Note	Desired Freq, Hz	Actual Freq, Hz	Division Ratio	Error, Hz	Error, %
C	261.63	261.629	38222	0.001	0.0004
C#	277.18	277.177	36078	0.003	0.001
D	293.66	293.659	34053	0.001	0.0003
D#	311.13	311.129	32141	0.001	0.0003
E	329.63	329.63	30337	0.000	0.000
F	349.23	349.235	28634	0.005	0.0014
F#	369.99	369.986	27028	0.004	0.001
G	391.99	391.987	25511	0.003	0.0007
G#	415.31	415.316	24078	0.006	0.0015
A	440.00	440.005	22727	0.005	0.001
A#	466.16	466.157	21452	0.003	0.0006
B	493.88	493.875	20248	0.005	0.001

played in reverse. And for the avid amateur composer, this is only one of hundreds of possibilities. The imagination can be quite useful in this respect.

Square waves can be the most generally useful waveform available. Not only are they simple to generate but they sound generally satisfactory when reproduced as single notes, they can be shaped, and they can be divided to produce a very wide spectrum of sound for many purposes.

Still using the ETS, Table 1-3 illustrates how a 10 MHz crystal-controlled oscillator signal might be divided to generate notes that could be used for piano tuning for example. The accuracy is far better than a tuning fork and the stability is as good as the crystal used.

The first column shows the note, the second the desired frequency, and the third shows the frequency obtained using the division ratio shown. The fifth column shows the error in hertz, and the final column the percentage error. Table 1-4 gives the binary equivalent for each division ratio which will help determine decoding for counter control.

The games one can play with even this rather simple system and modern logic tend to stagger the imagination. Some circuit details will be presented in the circuit construction portion of this text, but a preview may be in order. Four 4-bit counters can be forced to divide by 38222 by using the binary number shown to reset or clear the counter at a count of 38222.

Table 1-4. Binary Equivalents for Frequency Division Ratios.

DECIMAL FREQUENCY					BINARY EQUIVALENT
38222	1001	0101	0100	1110	
36078	1000	1100	1110	1110	
34053	1000	0101	0000	0101	
32141	0111	1101	1000	1101	
30337	0111	1110	1000	0001	
28634	0110	1111	1101	1010	
27028	0110	1001	1001	0100	
25511	0110	0011	1010	0111	
24078	0101	1110	0000	1110	
22727	0101	1000	1100	0111	
21452	0101	0011	1100	1100	
20248	0100	1111	0001	1000	

It is also worth noting that dividing the frequency is equivalent to multiplying the period. In this case the period of 10 MHz is 0.1 μsec, so the period after division is 0.0038222 second. The period for one cycle of 261.63 Hz is 0.00382219 second. If the output of a 16-input gate is used to cycle the counter to zero after 38222 counts, this same gate output can be used as the clock input to a single J-K flip-flop followed by one more divide-by-2 stage to generate a symmetrical square wave output at 261.629 Hz.

The result is an extremely accurate tuning source. The same principle could be used to generate the entire 9-octave frequency range, if desired.

Taking octave 7, lower C is 4186.01 Hz. The division ratio from a 10 MHz oscillator will be 2388.91 Hz. Rounding this to 2389 will generate a frequency of 4185.85 Hz, near enough to the desired frequency. Lower C for each lower octave can be obtained by dividing by two for each new note. The result would be a phase-locked organ in near-perfect tune, but such heroic efforts would probably be less than desirable from a musical standpoint. Advocates of phase-free organs contend that much of the character of music is lost when beat notes are eliminated in this way.

The 10 MHz oscillator frequency was chosen arbitrarily to illustrate a point. Other frequencies can certainly be used.

Figure 1-9 shows still another possibility. The ratio of 196 to 185 is 1.059459, quite near $\sqrt[12]{2}$. If a master oscillator is used for C, the B below and succeeding notes can be generated by dividing the master C by 196 and the lower B by 185.

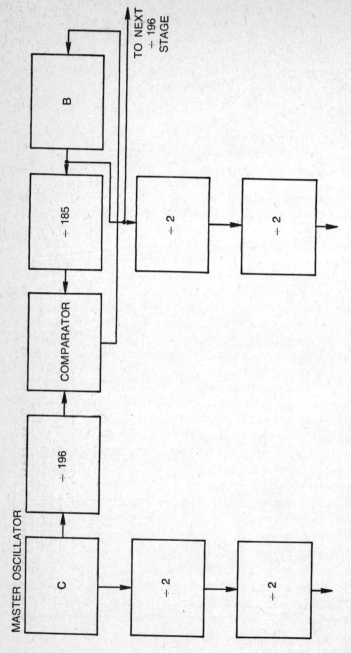

Fig. 1-9. Frequency division for master oscillator tone generation.

Comparing these will give a signal that can be used to lock the lower oscillator to the required ratio. Implementing this system with medium-scale integrated circuits requires a considerable amount of electronics, but the system is used in some organs and allows tuning the entire organ from a single control.

Additional digital synthesis systems are possible, and some using digital/analog (D/A) conversion techniques are in use. The entire waveform, including the envelope, is synthesized to achieve some remarkable results.

There are some simple circuits for the generation of tones by rudimentary forms of D/A conversion that will be shown in part 2. These make use of unijunction transistors and similar devices to generate sounds in the form of simple scales.

Also, a number of VCO and multivibrator circuits will be discussed and circuits shown to illustrate a variety of possibilities in sound sources. Figure 1-10 shows the programing tape used in a *very* complex RCA synthesizer. Any

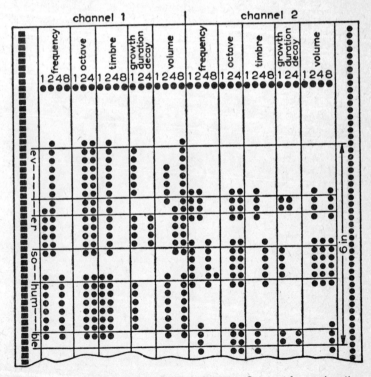

Fig. 1-10. Programing tape for RCA synthesizer. See text for explanation of use.

one of 16 frequencies in any of 8 octaves can be chosen by the first two columns of channel 1. Timbre is chosen by column 3, and the envelope shape by column 4, with overall volume chosen by column 5.

One of the more difficult types of sound to synthesize is that of various percussion instruments such as drums, cymbals, struck strings (piano) and so forth. These are normally composed of some fundamental frequency buried in a lot of noise. Even the noise will vary widely in spectrum content.

For most purposes it is easier to synthesize the individual sounds in hard-wired form than to develop them by programing a full synthesizer. A source of noise (a "noisy" zener diode), a heavily damped twin-tee or similar oscillator, an envelope shaper, and filter—however simple each part may be—are usually required for each sound, but the circuitry for as many as 8 percussion instruments takes up very little space.

Figure 1-11 is the waveform developed by the envelope shaper for a piano discussed in a subsequent section. In this case the key is pressed and released at 0.6 second without *sustain*. In Fig. 1-12, *sustain* allows the waveform to decay over nearly 1.4 seconds.

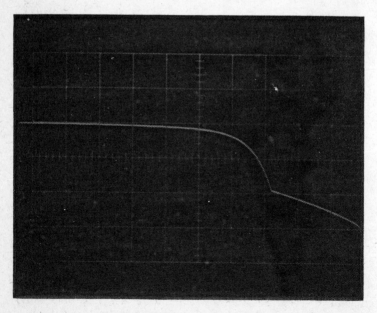

Fig. 1-11. Envelope shaper waveform (electronic piano).

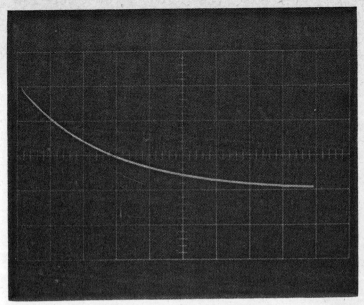

Fig. 1-12. Slow-decaying sustain.

Before proceeding to sound treatments, it will be worthwhile to preview some sound sources.

Microphone

Microphones of many types are available to pick up voice or instrumental sounds (Fig. 1-13A). Some very unusual effects can be obtained by mixing these inputs with others or by treating them in various ways. The room for experimentation is endless.

Tape Recorder

The production of many unusual and beautiful sounds can be achieved using a tape recorder (Fig. 1-13B). The Philips 4450 makes an ideal choice for echo effects, track-to-track recording, mixing, and so forth.

Sine-Wave Oscillator

Sine-wave oscillators alone do not make very desirable sources of sound, but they prove useful for *tremolo* in ring modulators and for mixing with other sounds to achieve specific results. (See Fig. 1-13C.)

Manual controls that could be incorporated include frequency control (tuning), amplitude control, and some means of keying. The keying could be applied to the V_{cc} line

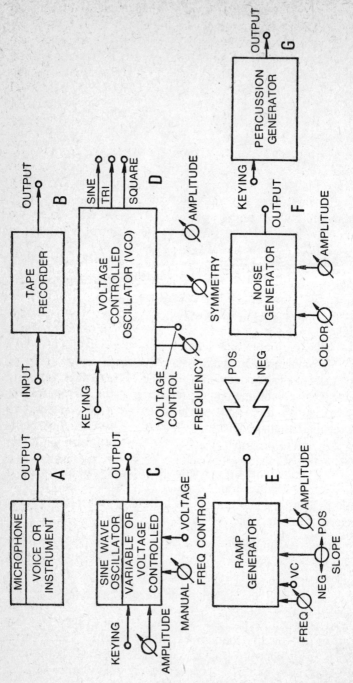

Fig. 1-13. Utilization of audio sources.

30

(applying either voltage or ground), but care must be taken under these circumstances to avoid the introduction of *key thumps* by softening the keying attack and decay with an appropriate RC network in the keying line.

If voltage control is used, it will only be necessary to control the frequency. Amplitude and keying control will be obtained elsewhere in the system. In other words, amplitude control will only be necessary or desirable as a manual control.

Voltage-Controlled Oscillator

The modern synthesizer VCO is shown in block form in Fig. 1-13D. The VCO is usually made available in pairs at least, and both of these may not have all of the outputs shown. The ability to achieve at least the triangular and square wave is simple enough to make it highly desirable to have *at least* these two outputs. The sine wave with symmetry control will make a tremendous repertoire of sounds available.

With symmetry control, the square wave can be anything from a symmetrical square wave to a very narrow pulse; the triangular wave will form anything from a good triangle to a ramp of either positive or negative slope. The sine-wave output can be either a good sine wave or what appears to be a full-wave rectifier output: sine pulses of either polarity.

The available harmonic content from such an array of outputs makes any music synthesizer a far more versatile instrument than if the outputs are abbreviated for the sake of economy. A good combination is two of these oscillators covering 20 to 10,000 Hz with a third covering 0.05 to 60 Hz (or a period of 20 seconds to 0.0166 second). This latter oscillator can be properly mixed with the ramp generator output to achieve a staircase for the generation of scales, arpeggios, and stepped *glides*.

A keying input should be available to allow this and other oscillators to be started in step. The symmetry control is used to change the triangular wave to a positive- or negative-slope ramp, the square wave to a positive or negative pulse, and the sine wave to positive or negative sine pulses.

The amplitude control is self-explanatory. The voltage control input will vary the output frequency over some predetermined range, while the center or starting frequency can be set by the manual frequency control. The manual frequency control should be a low-cost multiturn potentiometer or, better still, a high-quality 10-turn Helipot with a good turns-counting dial. Clarostat makes a small 10-turn potentiometer and a miniature dial that should prove ideal for this application.

An oscillator of this complexity will be somewhat costly to build, but the results should be worth the effort. Modular construction makes it possible to build the system up slowly. A modular cabinet with power built in and distributed to connectors is an ideal starting point.

The keyboard is a second desirable item. A 61-note keyboard with triple contacts can be connected to five 44-pin PC sockets to allow all of the keying connections to be made simply.

Ramp Generator

The ramp generator is used to sweep voltage control inputs through a selected range in a linear fashion (Fig. 1-13E). Applied to the VCO, a positive ramp will sweep the frequency of that oscillator from low to high and in the reverse direction for a negative ramp. Using a low-frequency positive ramp and a negative ramp of 12 times the frequency with amplitudes properly adjusted, a 12-note rising scale can be generated and repeated.

Again, the slope, amplitude, and frequency can be manually controlled and the frequency can be voltage-controlled. Some very unusual effects can be achieved by controlling the frequency of the ramp generator with the output from something like a high-frequency ramp or triangular wave.

It is possible to develop a trigger or keying pulse at the start of each ramp which could be used to start and stop a VCO. This can prove to be a most interesting arrangement.

Noise Generator

A noise diode, with the output properly amplified, makes an excellent source of *white* noise (Fig. 1-13F). The output can be filtered (the amount of filtering determined by the *color* and *amplitude* controls. The noise can be used alone or mixed with other sounds to produce a wide range of effects.

Percussion Generator

Many percussion instruments can be simulated with the sources already described, but it is useful to have a set of percussion generators triggered by the keyboard or a sequencer (Fig. 1-13G). The so-called *rhythm generators* are nothing more than sequenced percussion generator circuits.

The sequence is normally selected by a multiwafer rotary switch, but logic sequencing or actual programing with a bipolar memory system is possible (and is described later).

Pulse keying from logic or other sources, switch keying, or touch keying must be used to trigger the percussion generator. This action will, in the case of drums or other percussion instruments, trigger a ringing oscillator or start an envelope shaper. The resulting damped oscillations can be filtered to achieve the desired harmonic content and perhaps further damped to achieve the desired sound.

Bass drums, snare drums, bongos, and blocks may well use a ringing oscillator, since the output is largely a characteristic fundamental frequency with little noise. Cymbals require a fundamental with noise while a drum brush is practically all noise. It is possible to develop some very complex circuitry for any one or all of the generators. Keying and output levels are the only required inputs and outputs.

SOUND TREATMENT

A sound treatment can be any device that accepts an input from some source, modifies or treats it in some specific way, and supplies an output that is a result of the original sound and the treatment. The treatment may remove or add harmonics, alter the sound in amplitude, change the shape of the fundamental frequency, or any of a number of things. In this respect, a tape recorder can be considered both a sound source and a sound treatment. There are, however, several purely electronic treatments that are sufficiently useful or unusual to warrant developing circuits for them.

Filter

The most familiar filter to most people will be the tone control with treble and bass boost and cut. The normal arrangement is to have the treble boost/cut and the bass boost/cut as separate controls. A very useful circuit with four separate controls is included in the construction projects that follow.

Low-pass, high-pass, bandpass and bandstop filters, as well as specific tone-forming combination filters are very handy in electronic music. These can have some or all of the following controls; response, center frequency and output amplitude.

Voltage control could be applied to any one or all of these controls, but the center frequency is probably the only element worth controlling with voltage.

Reverberation

There are several types of reverberation systems available, but the one most used is probably the spring type in which an electrical transducer propagates a sound wave down a long mechanical metal spring. The delayed signal is picked up by another transducer and mixed with the original signal to produce a multiple echo effect.

The input can be any treated or untreated sound while the output will be the sound with multiple echos. Both the input and output levels can be controlled. Increasing the input above a certain level can cause distortion which, depending on the result desired, can be either good or bad. The output amplitude will determine how much of the reverberated sound is available to mix with the original sound, and the reverberation control will determine how much of each sound is actually made available at the output.

Where cost is no object, another type of echo system offers even greater latitude in creating effects. A tape loop with one or more record heads and one or more adjustable playback heads allows a precise echo effect to be achieved. This can be done with some modification to any simple recorder. A variable-speed capstan motor will make the range of effects even better.

Ring Modulator

The ring modulator will rarely be seen as a circuit. It has the rather unique ability to accept two inputs and give only the sum and difference as outputs.

Thus, with a DC voltage on one input and an audio signal on the other, the output level of the audio can be varied. With the DC voltage at zero, the output will be zero and so forth.

With sine-wave inputs of 400 Hz and 500 Hz, the output will be a mixture of 100 Hz (difference) and 900 Hz (sum) with the two original frequencies missing or highly attenuated. Using other waveforms will give even more unusual results. These account for a large number of the "way-out" sounds that typify synthesizer music.

Envelope Shaper

An envelope shaper is used to develop *attack*, *sustain*, and *decay* for control of any sound source. The characteristics of fast attack, practically no sustain, and rapid decay to simulate a struck piano string have been shown in earlier waveforms. This envelope shaper will be discussed later with circuitry and used in a small electronic piano which can be expanded.

The same effect but with far less overall control could be obtained from a ringing oscillator. This type of oscillator is shown later with circuit details for various percussion instruments, but the principle of envelope control is used here in a different but equally useful form.

The envelope shaper to be used in a synthesizer should have a very high degree of control; although one is enough to achieve a wide variety of effects, two would be even more desirable. The first requirement is a shaper. It must be possible to generate a positive ramp whose rate of rise and final level are accurately controllable. The level reached should be held for a controllable length of time; the rate and duration of the negation of the idle period should be controllable (for a free-running shaper) or be capable of staying off until keyed (for a keying mode of operation).

In this latter respect, each segment of the envelope should be controlled by a one-shot multivibrator for duration control, and the attack and decay should have ramp *rate* controls. The resulting waveform can be used on its own for the voltage control of other circuits.

To insure that the sound does not "leak through" during the off time of the shaper, the input level should be under adequate control. Also, some of these parameters could be put under voltage control, but the desirability of this seems minimal.

Mixer and Multicoupler

These devices complement each other. The mixer can accept inputs from several different sources, mix them in desired proportions, and supply the result to a single output line. The inputs may be mixed via simple potentiometers, but cross coupling the various inputs through the resistance of the potentiometers is to be avoided.

The ideal mixer uses field-effect transistors as impedance-matching source-follower amplifiers on each input to eliminate the danger of cross coupling. The result also allows easy control of each individual input and the total output.

SOUND REPRODUCTION

The temptation is always there to use the family hi-fi system for experiments with various sound-producing devices. Be forewarned that you will end up pulling your hair out if you go that route.

In the first place, conventional stereo systems are decidedly unportable. It would leave a hole in the decor and gain you nothing but abuse. And even if you leave it in place and try to cable to it, you will find the connections you want to get at peculiarly inaccessible. And this is not to mention the problem of cables strewn across the living room or family room floor. Find a room you can experiment in without interruption—a bedroom, corner of the attic, garage or basement—anywhere that other members of the family seldom visit.

Put up a steel door or use bolts. Hang DANGER—HIGH VOLTAGE signs around or do anything that will discourage meddling, because you're certain to learn quickly that keyboards, switches, knobs, and flashing lights do indeed attract an unusual amount of attention.

Two fairly good loudspeaker enclosures with a full complement of speakers are very useful. If they are new, remove and hide the grille cloths or distress them in some other unartful way that will make them unsuitable as furniture. Failing that, attach them to wall or floor with a good grade of epoxy cement or hang them from the rafters. The point is that your speakers should be as good as or better than the family hi-fi but unattractive enough to insure that they stay in your studio.

Next, obtain a new or used relay rack and mount power supplies and amplifiers with connections brought out to the *front* for easy access. Leaving the amplifiers open and relatively undecorated in a relay rack will insure their obscurity from neighbors, the family, and anyone else not sold on your hobby.

A keyboard, tape recorder, and workbench will complete the first steps for your studio. So let's see what we have... a set of speakers, amplifiers, and preamplifiers, with controls and connections brought out to the front for easy access and maximum utility. Also, stereo headphones for private listening will be useful (more likely, absolutely essential) when the studio is to be used so that it will not disturb others. If you play even a simple percussion generator or sine-wave oscillator through a small, low-wattage reproduction system, it will sound like noise to anyone but you.

An open-reel tape recorder, although it may seem expensive, is the next important outlay and it can help make a system the best or the worst, depending on quality and facilities. A good tape editing kit is another must, plus several loops of tape with facilities provided for guiding the loops.

2 | Experimenters' Circuits

We have already discussed the desirability of starting a studio setup with power supplies, reproduction equipment, a tape recorder, a keyboard, and perhaps a microphone.

We are going to develop a large number of sound source and sound treatment circuits that you can build in breadboard form for testing. This will give you an opportunity to test the various circuits for suitability in your own studio setup before committing them to some permanent form.

BASIC SOUND SOURCES

A conventional amplifier with regenerative feedback becomes an oscillator that can be used as the source for electronic musical sounds. Similarly, a pair of transistors connected into a switching circuit forms a multivibrator that creates musical sounds.

Multivibrators

We start with multivibrator circuits. The information here shows how to tune these circuits, how to use them with voltage control, 'and how to combine them with existing studio equipment to develop some very interesting and novel musical effects.

The simple free-running multivibrator of Fig. 2-1 makes an excellent starting point for discussions about multivibrators as sound sources.

First, the selection of the collector load resistors R1 and R4 depend largely on the allowable current drain from the power supply. We begin by selecting a voltage—15V for the sake of discussion—and an allowable current drain of, say, 10 mA (0.01A); since each transistor is conducting roughly half the time, by Ohm's law R1 and R4 should be $15/0.001 = 1500\Omega$.

Another factor that might be considered is the switching time of the multivibrator. This is determined by the size of the collector load resistor and the capacitor, since the capacitor

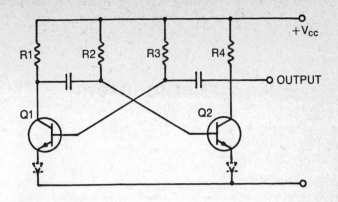

Fig. 2-1. Free-running multivibrator circuit.

must discharge through the load resistor during switching. Using 8000 Hz as the upper frequency of interest (Table 1-1) we can determine a period for one cycle of about 120 μsec or 60 μsec for one-half cycle.

If we arbitrarily decide that the rise time should take no more than about 10% of this period, we arrive at a switching time of 6 μsec. It takes roughly 5 time constants for a complete amplitude change, which means that the time constant of the collector load resistor and coupling capacitor should not, if possible, exceed 1 μsec. The time constant, of course, is equal to the product of resistance and capacitance. So, by dividing the time constant in seconds (0.000 001) by the resistance in ohms (1500), we arrive at the capacitance value we need: 667 pF.

We can calculate the required value of R2 and R3 by dividing the full-cycle period of an 8000 Hz note (about 120 μsec) by the calculated capacitance (667 pF).

$$\frac{0.00012}{0.000\ 000\ 000\ 667} = 89,950\Omega$$

The nearest commonly available value is 82K. This is the best way to calculate the various requirements and arrive at values close enough to produce a decent square wave at the desired frequency. Cut-and-try experimentation can be used to optimize performance from this point.

The circuit just described was built on a breadboard using the calculated values of resistors and 690 pF, 5% silver-mica capacitors to determine the accuracy of the calculations. Figure 2-2 shows the resulting square wave on the collector of Q2 with V_{cc} set at 10V (emitters grounded).

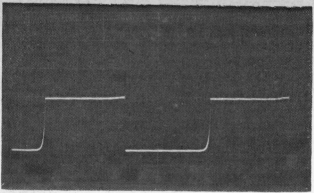

Fig. 2-2. Oscilloscope photo of square wave as obtained from Q2 collector (Vcc = 10V).

The first thing to note is that it is a good, symmetrical square wave with a rise time of less than 10% of the period of one-half cycle. But it rings quite badly on the negative excursion as Q2 is turning on. The reverse voltage being applied to the base—emitter junction of Q1 probably exceeds the breakdown voltage of that junction. So it is a good idea to install a diode with a peak inverse voltage rating of at least twice the value of V_{cc} to eliminate this problem. Figure 2-3 shows the resulting waveform.

The frequency for the waveform of Fig. 2-2 is 8333 Hz; in Fig. 2-3 it is 7143 Hz. The result is close enough to tune to 8000 Hz with either two trimmer resistors or two fixed resistors tied together at the top and one trimmer to adjust the frequency, as in Fig. 2-4.

Choosing 440 Hz, the period comes out to 0.002273 second; and for 220 Hz (an octave spread), to 0.004545. Assuming a

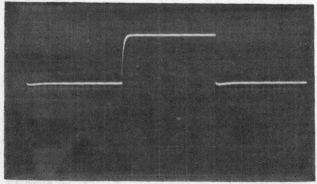

Fig. 2-3. Ringing is minimized with addition of diode to limit voltage at Q1 base—emitter junction.

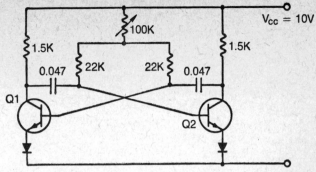

Fig. 2-4. A 100K trimmer adjusts the frequency of this multivibrator.

capacitor of 0.05 μF, the resistance for 440 is 45,460Ω and for 220 Hz it is 90,900Ω. Under these circumstances, a dual 100K potentiometer could be used to tune the entire octave. Or, if

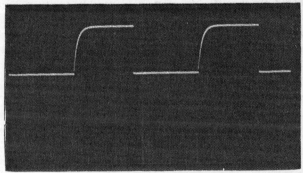

Fig. 2-5. Oscillator waveforms, 440 Hz.

distortion is not important, two 20K fixed resistors and one 100K potentiometer would tune the octave.

Figure 2-5 shows the waveform for 400 Hz (435) and Fig. 2-6 shows the waveform for 220 Hz (222.2). The latter

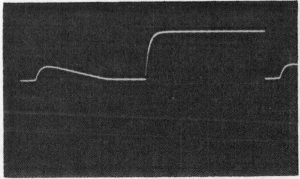

Fig. 2-6. Oscillator waveform, 220 Hz.

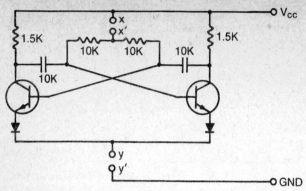

Fig. 2-7. Multivibrator with opens (x and y) for elements to be added to enhance versatility.

waveform is beginning to distort because of the interaction between the two transistors through the common potentiometers, but the result does not sound as bad as it looks.

There are a multitude of things that can be done with this versatile device. In Fig. 2-7 we have opened two places (x and y). The capacitors will depend on the frequency you want. The transistors can be any good NPN switching transistor; just be sure that the biases are properly applied.

The diodes can be any low-cost silicon type rated at twice V_{CC}. Now, between x and x', and variable resistance can be introduced to vary the frequency; and between y and y' any type of switch can be installed to turn the multivibrator on and off.

In Fig. 2-8A, a photocell is introduced between x and x'. This could be exposed to ambient light changes. It could be

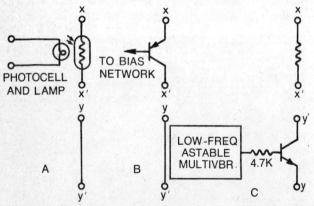

Fig. 2-8. Elements for plug-in at opens **x** and **y** of Fig. 2-7.

"played" with the hands, or it could be exposed to a tungsten lamp or light-emitting diode to which a varying voltage is applied to make a VCO.

In Fig. 2-8B, a transistor or FET can be put in the x' position and, properly biased, used to make a VCO. The circuit of Fig. 2-8C can be used as a wild alarm system. A reed relay could be used to apply power to the multivibrator, which will then allow the low-frequency oscillator to turn the high-frequency multivibrator on and off. And by applying the complementary output (the other collector) of the low-frequency multivibrator to another high-frequency multivibrator, a warbling siren results.

By adjusting the frequency of the three oscillators, you can mimic just about any siren going. And if asymmetry is introduced into any one or all of them, the results should prove "lease breaking" if not particularly gratifying from a musical standpoint.

Unijunction Oscillators

The unijunction transistor can be used as a fixed, variable, or voltage-controlled oscillator. It is about the most tolerant circuit in the world in that the component values can be almost anything and the circuit will still function. In the circuit of Fig. 2-9, the base 1 (B1) and base 2 (B2) resistors are made 22Ω and 220Ω, respectively. They could be interchanged or made anything from 10Ω to 1000Ω with little change in circuit operation.

The output from B1 is a positive-going spike as shown in Fig. 2-10. The output from B2 will be a negative spike, while the output from the emitter (E) is a sawtooth, as in Fig. 2-11. The sawtooth is the most useful waveform in terms of its use in

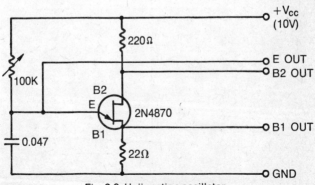

Fig. 2-9. Unijunction oscillator.

43

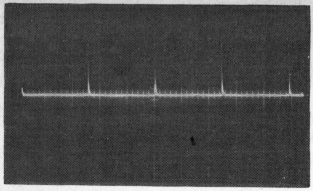

Fig. 2-10. Base-1 output of unijunction oscillator.

generating musical sounds. The frequency is about 440 Hz and the amplitude about 5V.

The buffer of Fig. 2-12 can be used to reduce the output impedance of the oscillator and to prevent frequency pulling under load. The waveforms for various types of *voicing* filters are shown in the waveform illustrations.

The first voicing filter (1, Fig. 2-12B) will give an output very similar to the form of Fig. 2-11. Figure 2-13 is the output obtained using (2) and Fig. 2-14 is the output obtained using (3).

It would be difficult to characterize these in terms of musical sounds such as *flute* or *oboe*, but they all have distinctive characteristics. The output obtained using (4) is shown in Fig. 2-15; the final waveform, Fig. 2-16, approximates a sine wave. In fact, increasing the size of one resistor will improve it even further. The final filter (6) can be

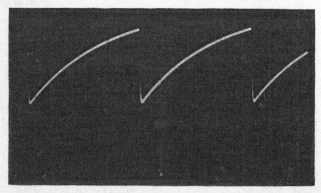

Fig. 2-11. Emitter output of unijunction oscillator.

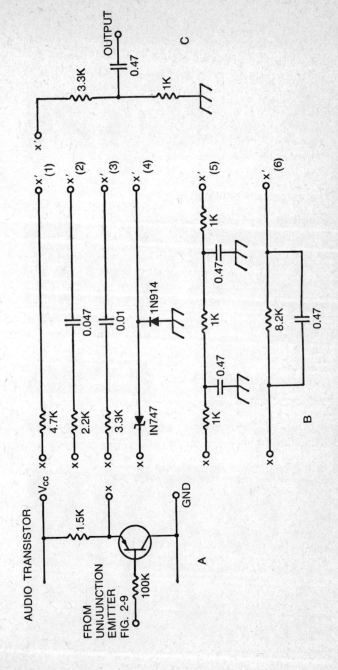

Fig. 2-12. Buffer circuit (A), RC voicing filter networks (B), and RC voltage divider voicing filter (C).

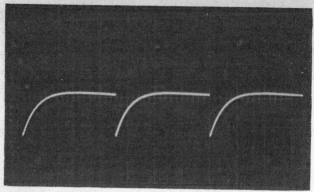

Fig. 2-13. Output waveform using voicing filter 2 of Fig. 2-12B.

used (with proper circuitry on the output) to give an overdriven signal simulating *fuzz*.

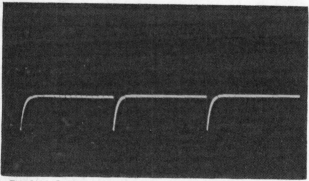

Fig. 2-14. Output waveform using voicing filter 3 of Fig. 2-12B.

With any of the systems described under multivibrators, this oscillator can be voltage-controlled. For example, in Fig.

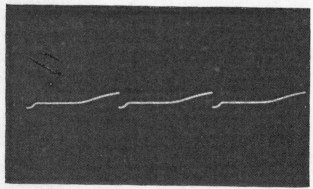

Fig. 2-15. Output waveform using voicing filter 4.

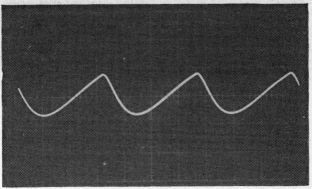

Fig. 2-16. Rough sine-wave output using voicing filter 5.

2-17 an extra charge path is made available through a 10K resistor to the variable input voltage. As the input voltage is increased, the time constant is decreased, shortening the period and increasing the frequency. In this particular circuit, with a capacitance of 0.68 μF, the frequency range is 670—4550 Hz; with 0.2 μF it is 220—1400 Hz.

Figure 2-18 makes use of a transistor as a variable resistor. Since the effect of varying the current in the base—emitter junction of a transistor is to vary the collector—emitter current by that amount times beta, the effect is a variable resistance in series with the capacitor.

In this case the input is AC-coupled. In Fig. 2-19, the input is DC-coupled, but the control voltage should be clamped to a +12V level and allowed to vary over a 12—20V range.

A novel tone-generating system is shown in Fig. 2-20. In this case the full 13-note range from C to C′ is delivered by

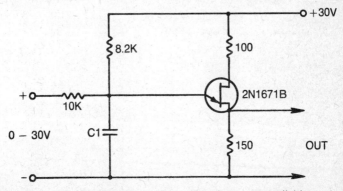

Fig. 2-17. Unijunction oscillator with voltage controllable output frequency.

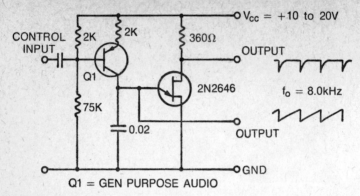

Fig. 2-18. Unijunction oscillator using bipolar transistor as a variable resistor controlled by AC voltage.

varying the resistance in the emitter circuit of the unijunction. The 5K trimmer is used for fine tuning while the 25K potentiometer allows the overall output range to be changed over several octaves.

Incorporating Integrated Circuits

Figures 2-21 and 2-22 are voltage-controlled oscillators using digital logic gates. Experimentation with these two circuits could lead to the discovery of some novel effects. Figure 2-23 is a more sophisticated vco and will serve to show the desirable features for such a device.

Although music synthesizers require a large number of treatment circuits for real variety, the heart of such a system is the vco. This oscillator should, ideally, have square wave, triangular-wave, and sine-wave outputs. The variety of outputs can be increased by adding symmetry control; this will allow

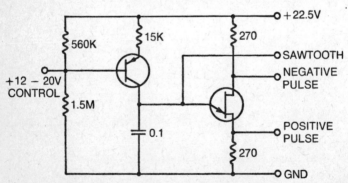

Fig. 2-19. Using low-voltage DC to vary bipolar transistor's resistance allows good control of unijunction oscillator frequency.

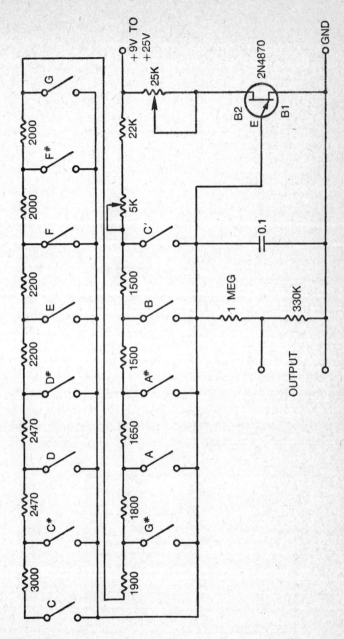

Fig. 2-20. Simple but effective switch-control system for changing oscillator frequency.

49

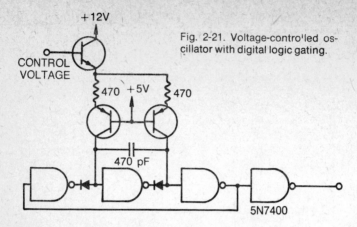

Fig. 2-21. Voltage-controlled oscillator with digital logic gating.

5N7400

for pulse and ramp outputs of either polarity. The circuit of Fig. 2-23 allows for most of these features, but does not produce a sine wave.

Basically, the modern VCO uses a pair of operational amplifiers. The first is a ramp generator that allows a capacitor to charge linearly to one voltage extreme or the other. Since the tendency for such a device is to charge the capacitor to one extreme or the other and lock up, a comparator is put on the output of the ramp generator to periodically change the direction of capacitor charge.

In the circuit shown, the ramp generator is a 741 operational amplifier. This very popular IC amplifier is internally compensated and simple to use. It also has a controlled upper frequency limit, which makes it unsuitable for the comparator section. At high frequencies the comparator must switch very quickly; so an *uncompensated* 709 operational amplifier IC is used for this section. The

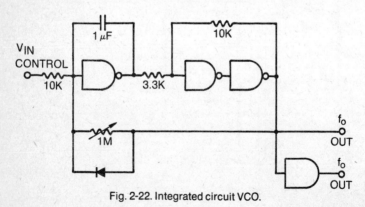

Fig. 2-22. Integrated circuit VCO.

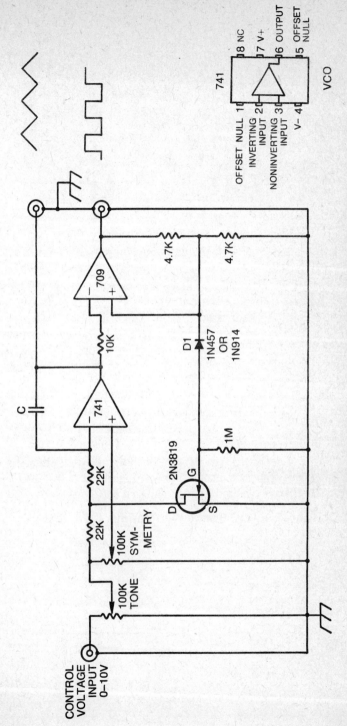

Fig. 2-23. Highly stable VCO for serious electronic-music application.

51

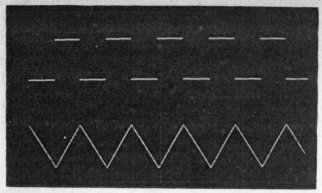

Fig. 2-24. Square and triangle waveforms as obtained from VCO of Fig. 2-23.

resulting square- and triangular-wave outputs are shown in Fig. 2-24.

The 100K tone control could be a 10-turn potentiometer for very precise control of the center frequency. The symmetry control could be the same type of potentiometer; but less accurate control of symmetry is acceptable. The frequency range available with various capacitance values is shown in Table 2-1. As shown, several octaves can be covered with this VCO.

Figure 2-25 shows the outputs with the symmetry control set at the two extremes. Although this circuit has its share of disadvantages, it is worth experimenting with in that it can be built very inexpensively.

One problem with the circuit is that the input must be positive with respect to ground; unfortunately, it is frequently desirable to have a nonpolarized input to a VCO.

Table 2-1. VCO Range With Various C Values.

	RANGE WITH 670 pF	RANGE WITH 1000 pF	RANGE WITH 0.01 μF
0	0		
1	812	519	35
2	1561	1000	110
3	2272	1470	159
4	2941	1887	207
5	3571	2380	251
6	4166	2702	293
7	4545	2941	320
8	5000	3226	352
9	5555	3571	390
10	5882	3846	413

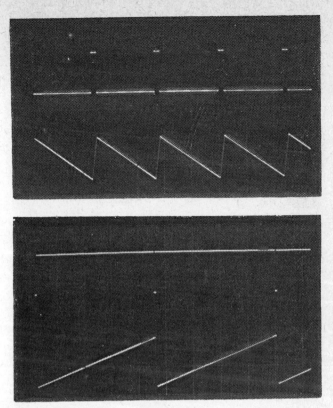

Fig. 2-25. Output waveforms with symmetry control set at extremes of range.

SOUND TREATMENT AND REPRODUCTION

Amplifiers are required frequently in the generation and shaping of the sounds used in electronic music. Figure 2-26 shows the circuit for an excellent low-noise amplifier using the 741 operational amplifier IC with a pair of input transistors. The output will be low impedance, as is required in most of these circuits; the input is AC-coupled.

Another frequent requirement is the mixing of sounds from different sources. Figure 2-27 illustrates a simple audio mixing arrangement. Unfortunately, such a mixer will frequently cause interaction of the two input circuits connected to it. Great care must be exercised when using such a mixer, and it should not be employed except as a temporary expedient. Figure 2-28 shows a mixer which, because of the high input impedance, will cause less interaction between the sources; and it has the advantage of using only two

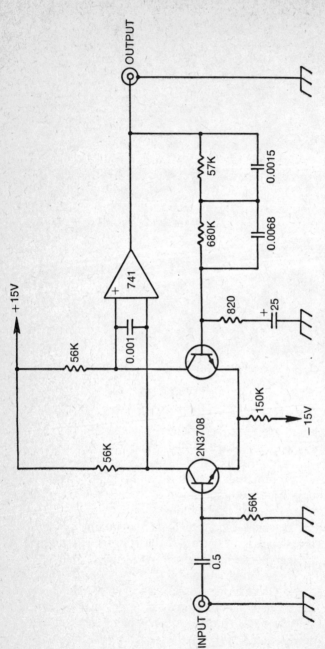

Fig. 2-26. 741 opamp as low-noise amplifier.

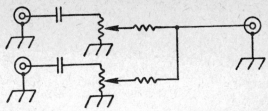

Fig. 2-27. Simple resistive audio mixer. This circuit is satisfactory for experimental purposes, but should not be employed in synthesizer because of excessive circuit loading that occurs when several sources of moderate impedance are coupled to a single input.

transistors, which will keep the cost down. The first transistor, a Motorola FET, is connected as a source follower, which offers an extremely high input impedance so that little circuit loading occurs despite the number of audio sources. The bipolar transistor, a conventional common-emitter amplifier, provides substantial gain.

The best mixer for most circumstances will be the one shown in Fig. 2-29. This mixer uses an input FET for *each* source, thus allowing the maximum separation of sources. The drains of these transistors are tied through a common drain

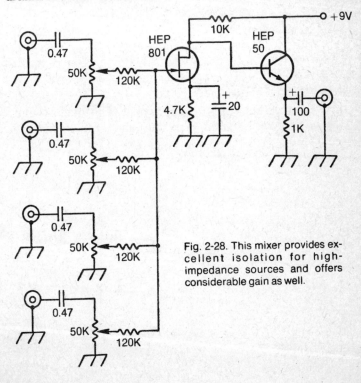

Fig. 2-28. This mixer provides excellent isolation for high-impedance sources and offers considerable gain as well.

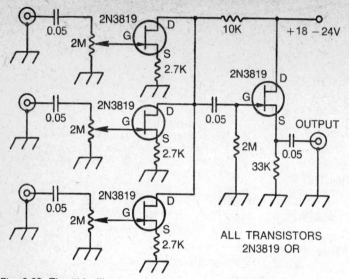

Fig. 2-29. The "ideal" mixer shown here offers almost infinite isolation between sources. The output FET is a source follower for optimum impedance matching.

resistor and the result is applied to the second-stage FET source follower to reduce the output impedance and contribute even further to the overall isolation of the sound sources.

Another possibility is the IC mixer of Fig. 2-30. Where a large number of 741 operational amplifiers are being used, this might be the ideal solution for most mixing problems, but it lacks the separation of the previous mixer and does not allow individual control of the sound sources.

Another possibility is the requirement of feeding several devices from a single source. In this instance a multicoupler is

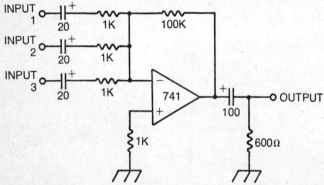

Fig. 2-30. Integrated circuit mixer offers performance comparable to circuit of Fig. 2-28.

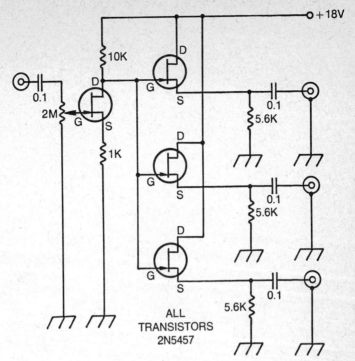

Fig. 2-31. A multicoupler is the reverse of a mixer—it allows several circuits to be fed from a single source without loading or circuit interaction.

a useful device. Such a circuit is shown in Fig. 2-31. The principle, again, is isolation of the driven devices from each other and from the source.

Still on the subject of treatments and reproduction, the circuits of Figs. 2-32 and 2-33 could be useful in a synthesizer

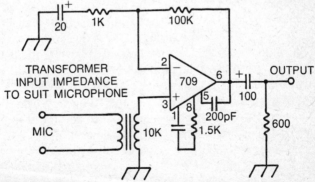

Fig. 2-32. The 709 integrated circuit as a microphone preamplifier.

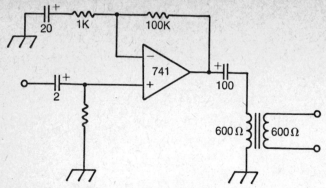

Fig. 2-33. Integrated circuit line amplifier for matching audio sources to a 600Ω line.

studio. The first is a microphone amplifier using a properly compensated 709 operational amplifier. The output impedance of the transformer should be 10K and the input impedance should be chosen to suit the microphone.

Figure 2-33 is a line amplifier which could be useful for driving 600Ω audio lines where the distance is further than a few feet.

Figure 2-34 shows the circuit of a voltage-countrolled filter. This is a device in which the center frequency of a bandpass filter can be controlled by an input voltage from something like a panning potentiometer (panpot), a device we'll be meeting in a later section. It is shown here mostly for illustration and for the experimenter who would like to build it, modify it as desired, and include it in a music studio. The design formula and a rough curve are included for information.

Tremolo is the variation of the amplitude of a sound at something around 7 Hz. The output can be applied to a vco or mixed with another sound source; it allows the control of both tremolo rate and depth. The rate is the 7 Hz, while the depth controls the amount of amplitude variation applied to the sound source. Figure 2-35 shows such a circuit. The HEP 251 is used as a twin-tee oscillator with variable frequency. The HEP 801 is used as a mixer for the sound source and the tremolo. (HEP-designated numbers are Motorola devices.)

For recorded sources, compensated amplifiers are frequently necessary. Figure 2-36 shows an RIAA-compensated (phono) amplifier while Fig. 2-37 shows the NAB-compensated (tape) amplifier voltage-controlled output

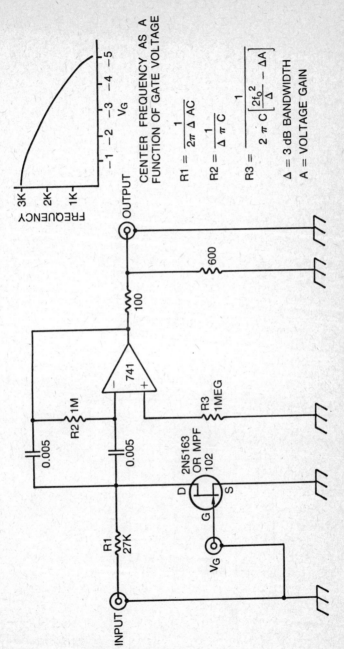

CENTER FREQUENCY AS A
FUNCTION OF GATE VOLTAGE

$$R1 = \frac{1}{2\pi \Delta AC}$$

$$R2 = \frac{1}{\Delta \pi C}$$

$$R3 = \frac{1}{2\pi C \sqrt{\left[\frac{2f_0^2}{\Delta} - \Delta A\right]}}$$

Δ = 3 dB BANDWIDTH
A = VOLTAGE GAIN

Fig. 2-34. Voltage-controlled filter.

59

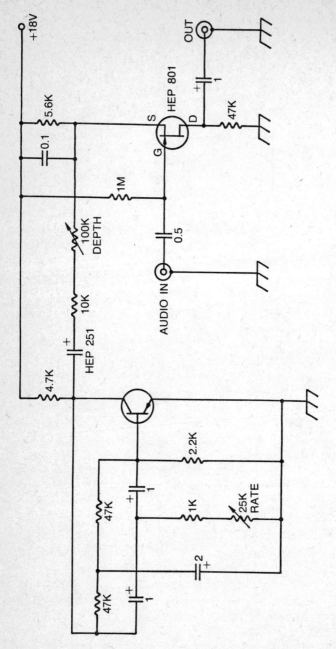

Fig. 2-35. Controllable tremolo circuit.

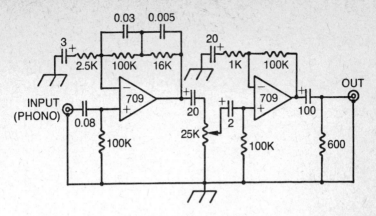

Fig. 2-36. RIAA-compensated amplifier.

level. In this case, a Raytheon CK1104P is used to control the gain of the 709 amplifier. Varying the intensity of the lamp (pins 1 and 2) changes the resistance of the photoresistor (pins 4 and 5). The output matches a 600Ω audio line.

A simple tone control is shown in Fig. 2-38. Far more sophisticated filters are described later; this circuit can be used for simple effects and for general tonal control of bass and treble.

Figures 2-39 through 2-42 illustrate several sources for producing percussion effects. All of these circuits are basically twin-tee oscillators which are set just below the point where they will go into self-oscillation. In Fig. 2-39 a switch at the input allows the circuit to be keyed. The 5K resistor (R11) is set just below the point where oscillation is sustained when the switch is pushed. Adjustment of this control will give a very realistic bass drum sound.

The twin-tee values can be varied to give a variety of drum sounds. The circuit of Fig. 2-40 gives a sound much like tom-toms; that of Fig. 2-41 offers still higher pitch to simulate bongos. Figure 2-42 is a circuit for a source that sounds like wood blocks or claves. A simple switch (Fig. 2-43) will allow any of these circuits to be driven from digital logic signals. Figure 2-44 shows a universal amplifier.

A novel device is the touch switch bongos shown in Fig. 2-45. The touch plates (shown as squares) will, when touched with the fingers, trigger the oscillator with which it is associated.

Although it is not adaptable to music synthesizers, the *wah-wah* circuit is worth including for experimentation.

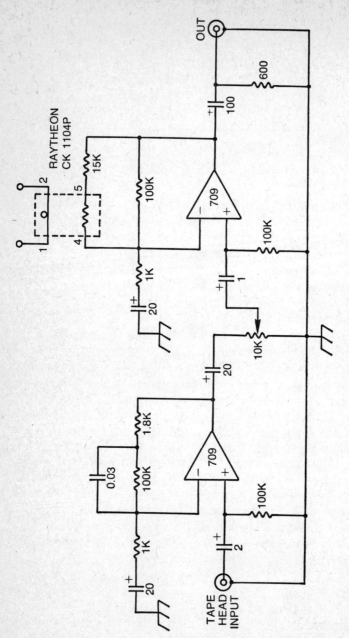

Fig. 2-37. NAB-compensated amplifier.

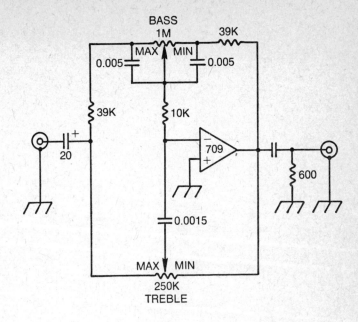

Fig. 2-38. Integrated circuit amplifier with bass and treble controls.

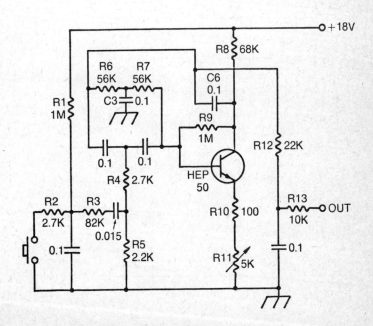

Fig. 2-39. Percussion generator with pushbutton for keying.

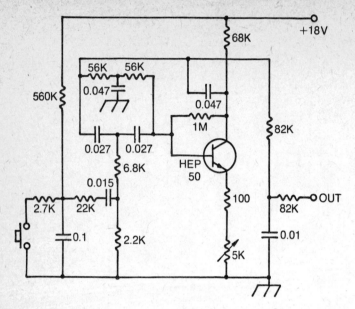

Fig. 2-40. Tom-tom percussion generator circuit.

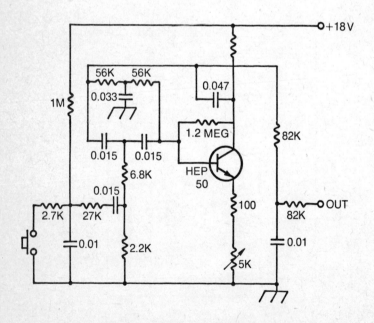

Fig. 2-41. Bongo percussion generator circuit.

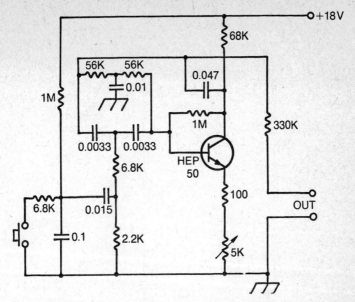

Fig. 2-42. Percussion generator that produces sound similar to wood blocks or claves.

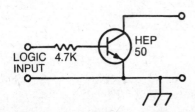

Fig. 2-43. Transistor switch will key percussion generators when driven with DC control voltage.

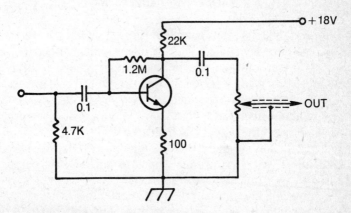

Fig. 2-44. General purpose amplifier for use with any of the sound source circuits presented in this book.

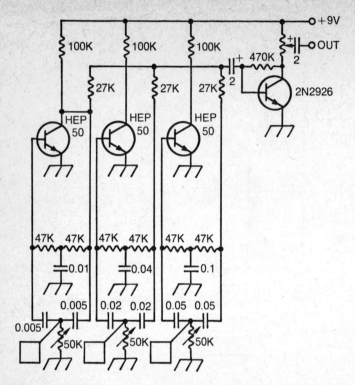

Fig. 2-45. Novel electronic bongo circuit uses touch plates to key individual generators.

Basically, the effect is achieved by using a variable bandpass filter. The bandpass characteristic is controlled with a foot pedal attached to a potentiometer (the variable resistance in the circuit of Fig. 2-46).

Figure 2-47 is the complete circuit diagram for a reverberation system using a spring line. Although much more complex reverberation effects and longer delays can be achieved with a tape recorder, this circuit serves in most music synthesizers to achieve a reasonably good reverberation effect. Later circuits will allow for the control of both the level of the output and the depth of the reverberation. The depth is nothing more than the amount of reverberation signal mixed with the original input to achieve the output desired.

Figure 2-48 shows a simple ring modulator. Basically, a ring modulator output consists of the sum and difference frequencies of the input signals, while the input signals themselves are eliminated or very much attenuated.

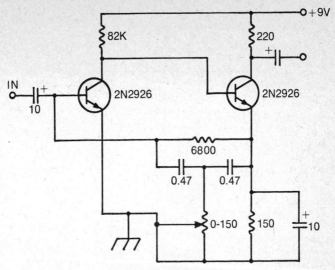

Fig. 2-46. Wah-wah circuit.

Figure 2-49 illustrates a slightly more sophisticated tone control circuit. In this circuit, general-purpose audio PNP and NPN transistors will serve very well.

The circuit features low distortion and good control and is, therefore, worth assembling for experimental purposes or for inclusion in a working synthesizer.

SYNTHESIZING NATURAL SOUNDS

The term *noise* probably makes most people think of jackhammers or trash cans being knocked together at 5 a.m.; but to the electronics buff noise has such a totally different meaning that it even comes in colors. *White noise* describes a signal which contains all possible frequencies from subaudio up through radio and microwave to gamma rays and beyond. *Pink noise* differs from white noise in that the probability that the signal contains a frequency outside the audio spectrum is very low.

The Wind

Pink noise should be particularly interesting to the audio experimenter because there are a lot of sounds that can only be produced using a noise source. In speech synthesis, sibilants and fricatives can't be produced without broad-spectrum noise. In music, snare drums and cymbals are only two examples of noise-based sounds. Finally, many natural phenomena such as the sound of the surf and the wind

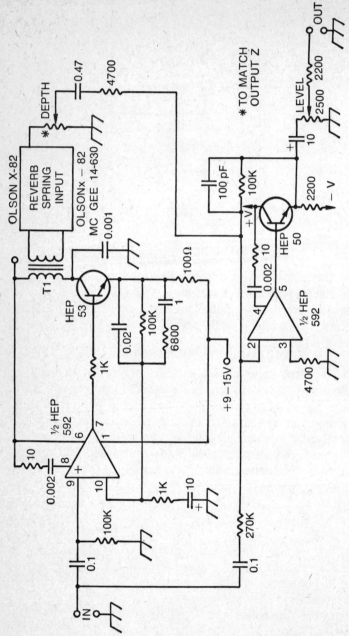

Fig. 2-47. Complete reverb system.

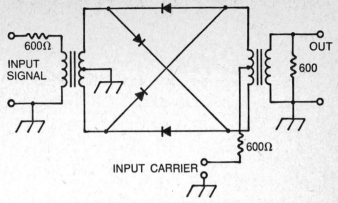

Fig. 2-48. Simple ring modulator.

are relatively easy to produce using noise that has its frequency content and amplitude varied randomly.

Testing and Operation. The *wind* sound source circuit is shown in Fig. 2-50. About the only important comment is that Q7 should be inherently noisy (note its open collector lead). Transistors Q1 through Q6 are 2N5129s; Q7 is a 2N2712. Transistors Q8 and Q9, respectively, are 2N2712 and 2N3391.

When you are sure that all components are properly installed and you've checked polarities of diodes and electrolytics, snap two fresh 9V batteries into the battery connectors.

Connect the output of the wind source into one of the high-level auxiliary inputs of a hi-fi or instrument amplifier and turn both the wind circuit and amplifier on. With R32 and R31 set to the approximate center of their rotation, you should hear a wind-like sound from the amplifier.

Trimmers R31 and R32 are both set according to personal preference, but a few general comments will get you started. R31 controls the amount of random voltage applied to the tuning input of the voltage-controlled filter. As this control is rotated clockwise the variability of the wind is increased. R32 controls the gain of the amplifier used in the bandpass filter and consequently the Q of the filter. Rotating R32 clockwise produces a shriller sound. A functional block diagram for the wind sound source is shown in Fig. 2-51.

Design Analysis. It is convenient to break the unit down into a noise source, voltage controlled bandpass filter (VCF) and a random voltage generator as shown in Fig. 2-51. These sections may be analyzed one at a time.

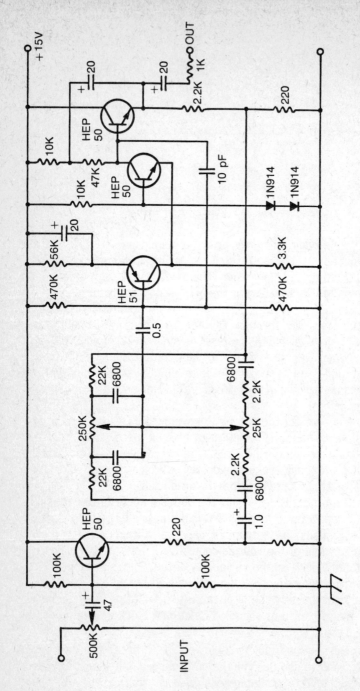

Fig. 2-49. Tone control circuit with signal isolation and impedance-matching stages.

70

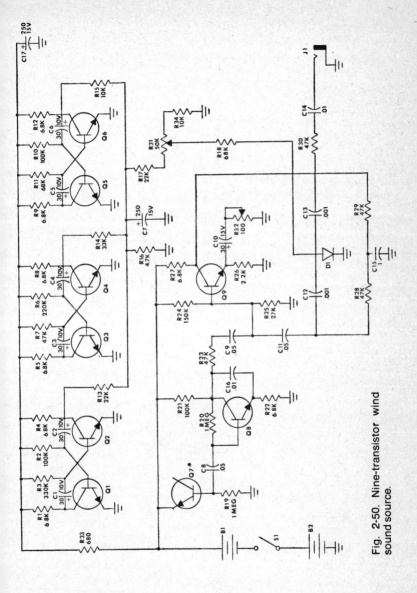

Fig. 2-50. Nine-transistor wind sound source.

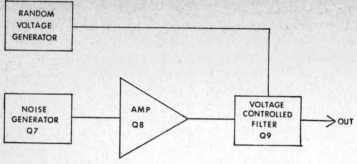

Fig. 2-51. Functional block diagram, wind simulator.

The noise source is built around a reverse-biased PN junction operating above its breakdown potential. The shot noise resulting from the avalanche breakdown mechanism of the reverse-biased base—emitter junction of Q7 is amplified by Q8 and passed on to the VCF circuit for voicing.

Control voltages for the VCF originate in the random voltage generator which consists of three astable multivibrators (Q1—Q6) running at different rates with different duty factors. The outputs of the three astables are summed with resistors R13, R14, and R15 and appear across R16. While the voltage appearing at this summing junction is to a certain extent random, it is weighed by the different values of the summing resistors and the different periods and duty factors of the astables to approximate the blowing of the wind. After being smoothed by the integrating action of the summing resistors and C7, the output of the random voltage generator is applied to the VCF.

The voltage controlled bandpass filter consists of a single transistor gain stage (Q9) with a parallel tee-notch filter in the feedback loop. For signals outside the notch frequency, insertion loss is very low so that these signals pass from the output of the amplifier back to the input with little attenuation.

However, since the output of the gain stage is 180° out of phase with respect to the input, the overall effect is one of negative feedback, resulting in the cancellation of the two signals. Signals that are within the notch frequency are attenuated by the filter so they produce no negative feedback and the amplifier passes them. R32 varies the amount of amplification provided by the gain stage and thereby controls the Q of the filter.

The nonlinearity of diode D1 makes it an ideal "variable resistor" to vary the center frequency of the notch filter. As the control voltage rises it applies a greater forward bias to D1, causing the diode's equivalent impedance to decrease. As the equivalent impedance at the junction of C12 and C13 increases the center frequency of the notch filter gets higher.

Figure 2-52 shows the layout for the commercial version of this circuit.

Steam Whistle

Even if model railroading is not one of your hobbies, you probably have a place in your studio for an authentic-sounding steam whistle. You couldn't get any closer to the sound of a real locomotive even if you bought ol' 99 and rolled her into your living room.

Operation. There are no adjustments which must be made to the whistle (Fig. 2-53) to make it operate, but there are a couple of component values you may want to trim out for what you consider to be the best sound.

The values of C1, C2, and C3 determine the pitch of the whistle. Using 0.005 μF for all three of these capacitors produces a high-pitched scream similar to European trains, while the use of 0.05 μF discs gives the roar of American freights. The three capacitors need not be of equal value in order to sustain oscillation; pitches between these two extremes can be produced by changing the values of one or more of these capacitors.

The amount of "steam" may be varied by altering the value of R7. For more noise, the value of this resistor may be decreased and for less hiss it's value increased.

Operation of the whistle is simply a matter of snapping two fresh 9V batteries into the battery connectors and plugging the output lead into the input of a suitable amplifier. Hi-fi, musical instrument, or even battery-powered amplifiers may be used; but bear in mind that the quality of the sound depends on the quality of the amplifier used.

Design Analysis. Reduced to basics, a whistle is nothing more than a resonant chamber which produces a tone when excited by the steam flowing over a turbulence-producing orifice. It would be nice if that were all there were to it—but it's not. There is also the sound of the steam which can be heard as a faint hiss as the whistle is blown. Also, like any other musical instrument, a whistle has its own peculiar attack and decay characteristics. That is, it takes a short time for the sound to build up to a maximum and the vibrations

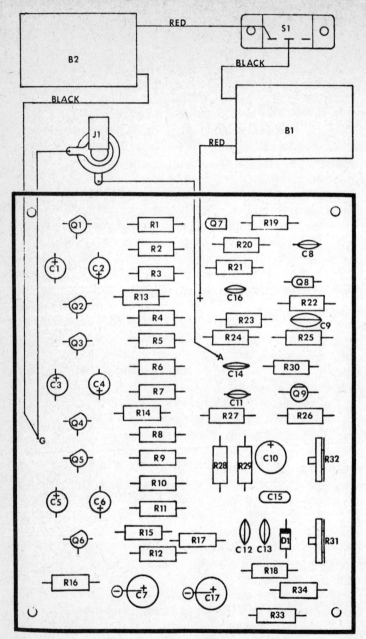

Fig. 2-52. Wind source circuit board. (Layout is from PAIA's production model.)

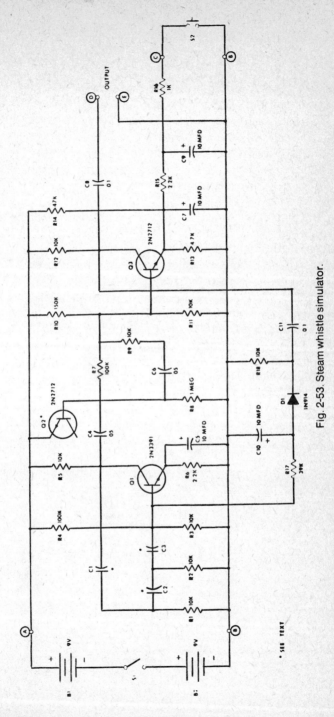

Fig. 2-53. Steam whistle simulator.

persist for some short time after the exciting force (steam) is removed. Finally, there is a slight lowering of pitch as the vibrating medium in the cavity changes from air to a denser air/water combination.

For ease of analysis the whistle may be divided into three essentially independent sections; an oscillator, noise source, and gating amplifier.

The oscillator is a standard phase-shift design with Q1 in a common-emitter configuration for gain and 180° of the required 360° phase shift. The remaining 180° of phase shift is provided by the frequency-determining components (C1, C2, C3, R1, R2, and R3).

Noise is provided by Q2, an inexpensive silicon NPN transistor which has its base—emitter junction biased above the junction's breakdown potential. The shot noise of the resulting avalanche breakdown mechanism appears across R8 and is used to simulate the sound of steam.

The outputs of the oscillator and the noise source are mixed by resistors R7 and R9 and applied to Q3. When pushbutton S2 is open Q3 cannot pass audio because its emitter is held at a slightly higher voltage than its base by the voltage divider R14 and R13. When S2 is closed, the voltage at Q3's emitter begins to drop as C9 discharges through R16.

As Q3's emitter voltage drops its base—emitter junction becomes more and more forward-biased, thereby increasing

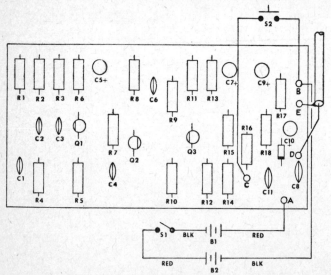

Fig. 2-54. Circuit board layout of steam whistle simulator.

the gain of Q3. When S2 is opened, a reverse action occurs as C9 charges through R15.

These two time constants are chosen to simulate the attack and decay characteristics of a real steam whistle.

Part of the output signal is tapped off of Q3's collector and rectified and filtered by D1 and C10. The resulting DC voltage is applied to Q1's base, where it gradually lowers the pitch of the oscillator slightly as the whistle is blown.

Figure 2-54 illustrates the layout of the commercial version of the steam whistle simulator.

The Surf

One of the most relaxing sounds imaginable is the roar of the surf. Anyone who is close enough and has the time heads for the seashore when he wants to unwind.

But what is really nice to have is the sound of the surf always available at the flick of a switch. And certainly no electronic-sound studio is complete without surf simulation.

The surf synthesizer is actually a special-purpose electronic music synthesis system. As depicted in Fig. 2-55, white noise generated by an inexpensive silicon transistor is voiced by a voltage-controlled low-pass filter and attenuator under the control of a random voltage generator to convincingly reproduce the sound of the breakers washing against the shore.

Setup and Operation. The only adjustments to be made to the surf synthesizer circuit (Fig. 2-56) are the settings of R34 and R45. While these settings are largely a matter of personal preference, a couple of tips will get you started. (Figure 2-57 shows a recommended board layout.)

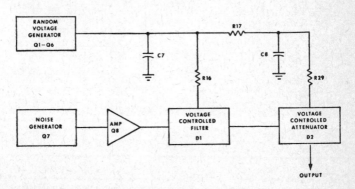

Fig. 2-55. Block diagram of system for simulating sound of surf.

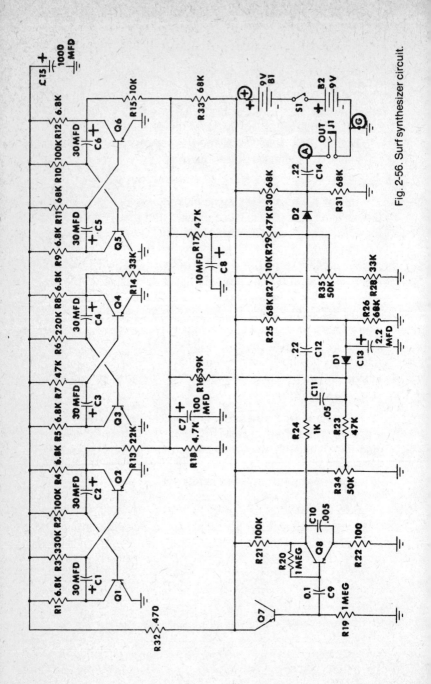

Fig. 2-56. Surf synthesizer circuit.

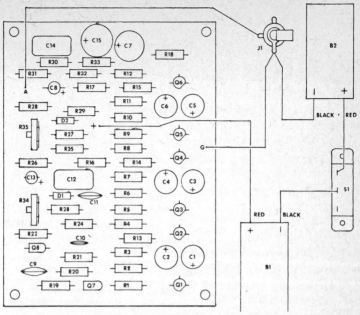

Fig. 2-57. Circuit board layout, surf synthesizer.

Connect the surf synthesizer to the amplifier you intend using and turn both on. Rotate R35 fully clockwise and adjust R34 for the widest and most natural sounding tone changes.

When you're satisfied with the adjustment of the tone control you can set R35 for volume changes. Adjustment of R35 is to your taste, but you will probably find that the most natural sound results when the synthesizer is completely muted for short periods. There is little electrical interaction between R35 and R34, but it will probably take some twiddling before you're completely satisfied with their adjustment.

Bear in mind that the quality of the amplifier used with the surf synthesizer will greatly affect the final sound. Select an amplifier with the best bass response available so that the roar of the surf can be heard as well as the crescendo-like crash as the waves break. It will probably be necessary to advance the amplifier's bass boost control to achieve a really natural sound.

When you have the surf synthesizer set up and operating, you will find it to be not only the greatest gadget in the world for relaxing but a great mood setter. As a conversation piece, it's unbeatable—no one will believe that a little bundle of electronics can make the sound of the ocean.

Design Analysis. The noise source is built around a reverse-biased PN junction operating above its breakdown potential. The shot noise resulting from the avalanche breakdown mechanism of the reverse-biased base—emitter junction of Q7 is amplified by Q8 and passed on to the VCF and VCA circuits for voicing.

Control voltages for the VCA and VCF originate in the random voltage generator, which consists of three astable multivibrators (Q1—Q6) running at different rates and with different duty factors. The outputs of the three astables are summed with resistors R13—R15 and appear across R18. While the voltage appearing at this summing junction is to a certain extent random, it is weighed by the different periods and duty factors of the astables and the different values of the summing resistors to approximate the roll of the ocean. After being smoothed by the integrating action, the output of the random voltage generator is applied to the VCF.

If there is a secret to the surf synthesizer it is the use of the VCF. When the VCA is disabled and only the VCF is operating the resulting sound will still be close to that of the surf even though there is no amplitude change. If, on the other hand, the VCA is working alone the result only sounds like interstation radio static fading in and out.

The VCF uses the nonlinear characteristics of a standard silicon diode as a voltage-controlled resistor. By proper adjustment of trimmer pot R34 diode D1 is ordinarily forward-biased, resulting in a loss of high frequencies through C11, D1, and C13. As the control voltage of the VCF increases, it reverse-biases D1 and allows less high frequency loss to ground. The high frequencies not shunted to ground naturally become part of the signal appearing at the output.

The action of the VCA is similar to that of the VCF in principle. D2 is inserted in series with the signal path and slightly reverse-biased by properly setting trimmer pot R35. As the control voltage applied to the anode of D2 increases, D2's effective resistance becomes less, thereby allowing more signal to pass to the output. Capacitor C12 serves only to block DC potential from the VCF stage and does not noticeably contribute to the overall frequency response of the device.

Sustain

Sustain is rapidly becoming one of the most often used accessories in the guitarist's bag of tricks—mainly because it is one of the few gadgets that has something to offer everyone.

Rock groups use sustain to give them biting attack and a cranked-up sound without blowing fuses, speakers, and eardrums. Beginners love the way sustain tends to fill in goofs that would otherwise come out as dead notes—and the way it compensates for the poor decay characteristics typical of inexpensive guitars. A good sustain also makes possible controlled feedback techniques that allow a note to be held literally indifinitely.

The *infinity plus* sustain circuit shown in Fig. 2-58 is not just a fuzz box hiding under the name of sustain and it's not just another tape compressor somebody decided to plug a guitar into. Designed from the ground up as a musical accessory, it features low noise, low distortion, fast attack and release time, and wide dynamic range. *Infinity plus* may seem like an ambitious name, but once you try it you'll agree that it fits. As Fig. 2-59 shows, the circuit doesn't command much layout space.

Setup and Operation. Use a small screwdriver to turn the adjusting slot on trimmer potentiometer R13 to about the midpoint of its rotation. Apply power to the sustain, plug your guitar into the input jack (J1), and jumper output J2 to the input of your amplifier. Set the volume at a moderate level and fully advance the guitar volume control.

Set *sustain duration* control S1 to the *out* position and strike a chord. If any distortion (fuzz) can be heard, reduce the guitar gain until it disappears. This setting of the guitar volume control is the optimum operating point for your instrument; make a mental note of the setting for future reference. Since there is considerable amplification by the sustain, this reduced setting of the guitar volume will not cause reduced total output from your amplifier. In fact, you will probably notice a slight boost in overall volume.

Very few pieces of special effects equipment are as easy to operate as the sustain. Clockwise rotation of the *sustain duration* switch increases the sustaining action. With the *sustain duration* control in the *out* position there is no sustain action and all guitar controls will operate normally. Unless fuzz is desired the guitar volume control should not be advanced beyond the optimum point determined above.

With the *sustain duration* control set to any of the sustaining positions, reducing the guitar volume below the optimum level will have the effect of reducing sustain duration. Any changes you may wish to make in overall

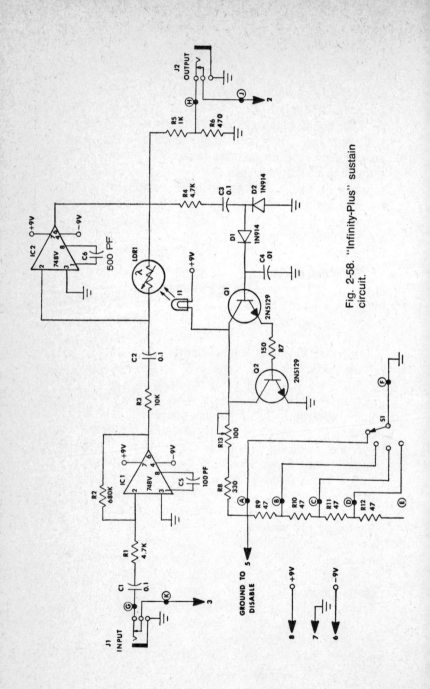

Fig. 2-58. "Infinity-Plus" sustain circuit.

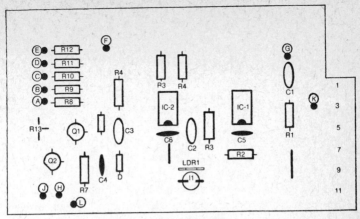

Fig. 2-59. Infinity-Plus circuit board layout.

volume while the sustain is in operation will have to be made at the amplifier controls.

One of the gimmicks you can try with the *infinity plus* is controlled feedback. Set *sustain duration* to maximum, guitar volume to optimum, and stand close to your speakers. Now strike a note and hold it. As the vibrations of the string die away the *infinity plus* will bring up the volume until the point is reached at which the sound regenerating in the amplifier is enough to keep the string vibrating. This resonant condition results in an infinitely sustained note; deadening the string is the only way to stop it.

As you become more familiar with the use of sustain you may notice that there is a slight sustaining action even when S1 is set to the *out* position. This can be corrected by clockwise rotation of the adjusting slot of internal trimmer potentiometer R13. Counterclockwise rotation of this control will cause an increase in the sustaining action of each of the settings of the *sustain duration control*.

Design Analysis. Operational amplifier (opamp) IC1 serves as both a preamp and impedance matcher. The gain of the second opamp is set by the internal resistance of photoresistor LDR1, which is in turn dependent on the illumination supplied by lamp I1. Part of the output of IC2 is tapped off by R4 and C3 and applied to the peak detector (D1, D2, and C4). The output of the peak detector is the input for the Darlington pair (Q1 and Q2), which drives lamp I1.

Assume that there is an input signal that is increasing in amplitude. As the signal at the output of IC2 tries to increase, it supplies a greater voltage to the peak detector, which turns on Q1 and Q2 to cause I1 to glow more brightly. When I1 gets brighter, it causes the internal resistance of LDR1 to decrease, which consequently decreases the gain and output of IC2. The net effect of this balancing act is that the output of IC2 stays practically constant. As in any feedback circuit, there is a slight error (feedback wouldn't work if there weren't), but thanks to the high gain of the Darlington pair, the error is minimal.

Resistors R8 through R13 serve a dual purpose. Most importantly they maintain a slight current flow through I1 at all times. This current keeps the filaments warm and minimizes the thermal inertia which would otherwise show up as considerable attack lag during the tremendous increase in signal when a guitar string is first plucked. Secondly, these resistors set the maximum system gain by setting a lower limit of illumination for I1. When S1 is in the *out* position there is a current path from I1 through R8 and R13 to ground. Under these conditions R13 can be adjusted so that the loudest anticipated passages cause no increase in illumination of I1; consequently, there is no sustain action and the guitar sound is natural. As more resistors in the chain (R9–R12) are switched in, the minimum brilliance of the bulb is lowered and the maximum gain of the amplifier is raised. As the maximum gain point is increased, the length of time the sustain can hold a note is increased.

The bridge-type power supply shown in Fig. 2-60 is adequate for the sustain circuit. The connector labeled 8 is the +V line; pin 6 is the −V terminal. Capacitors C1 and C2 should

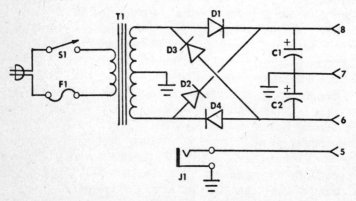

Fig. 2-60. Full-wave bridge power supply. Use plenty of capacitance for C1 and C2 (5000 μF each if possible).

be the highest-value electrolytics you have; in no case should these be lower in value than 2200 μF. The working-voltage rating of the electrolytics should be no less than 1.5 times the rated transformer secondary voltage.

Tremolo

For years some commercial electronic organs have used mechanical rotating speakers to produce a tremolo effect; recently, this offbeat approach has gained popularity with musicians in general because the sound produced is totally unlike most electronic forms of tremolo.

The problem with mechanical speakers is that they are bulky and much too heavy to be conveniently carried; and their high cost puts them beyond the means of many amateur and semiprofessional musicians. The tremolo circuit described in this section is a low-cost portable electronic device that simulates the rotating speaker effect. The manufacturer of the commercial version (see board, Fig. 2-61) calls it *Synthespin*.

Other than the rotating-speaker sound, the Synthespin can produce numerous effects ranging from very slow phasing type sounds to a bubbling pseudo-reverb. Electrical inputs provide for foot-pedal control of both speed and range of the rotating effect and allow instantaneous foot-switch cancellation and bypass functions.

Operation. The Synthespin is designed for low-level signal processing, so peak-to-peak signal amplitudes should in general be kept below 0.5V. When the unit is being used to process the signals from electrified musical instruments such as guitar, accordian, saxophone, etc. there is no problem as the signal levels from these instruments are typically considerably below this limit. When using the Synthespin with an electronic organ, however, the insertion point must be carefully chosen. An organ with an *expression* pedal offers the

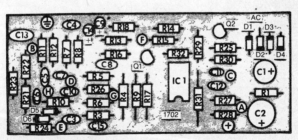

Fig. 2-61. Synthespin circuit board layout.

easiest possible installation because the connections to this pedal are often made with RCA-type phono connectors. It is a simple matter to unplug the input to the expression pedal and extend the lead by a sufficient amount to reach the location of the Synthespin unit. On organs that do not have expression pedals, the Synthespin may be inserted between the organ's preamplifier and power amplifier. This may require that small modifications be made inside the organ (to gain access to the preamp output).

You may find that you do not need to advance the volume controls of the instrument or amplifier quite as far when using the Synthespin. This is normal and is caused by a slight power boost designed into the Synthespin.

Operation of the controls as labeled on the schematic of Fig. 2-62 is as follows:

The apparent speed of the "rotating speaker" is variable from one cycle every three seconds to 15 per second using the SPEED control. Rotating the knob in a clockwise direction increases the speed.

The ACCENT control allows the performer to alter the presence of the Synthespin effect. As the control is rotated in a clockwise direction the effect becomes more pronounced. After some experimenting with the Synthespin you may notice that as the SPEED control is advanced the effect becomes more noticeable and a lower setting of ACCENT will produce an equivalent sound. This phenomenon is purely subjective; there is no interaction between these controls.

The SPAN control is also connected to the power switch; rotating the control fully counterclockwise turns the power off.

With the SPAN control at its fully clockwise setting, the CENTER control has no effect; but as SPAN is turned back, the CENTER control has a greater effect on the portion of the instrument's tonal range that is modified. When the SPAN control is fully off, the CENTER control can be used to manually phase the signal.

Closing a switch plugged into the CANCEL jack turns off the effect. Best results are obtained using a push-on/push-off switch such as that in the PAIA 4720 foot switch. (Throughout this book I refer to PAIA modules, special components, and systems. PAIA is the name of the synthesizer manufacturer that supplied not only the majority of working circuits published herein but much of the operating information, design analysis, and performance data. Specifically

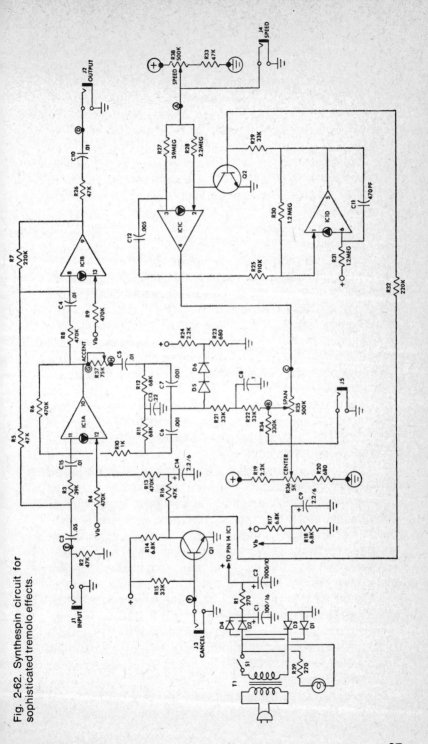

Fig. 2-62. Synthespin circuit for sophisticated tremolo effects.

87

referenced components, foot switches, keyboards, and completely wired and tested circuit modules may be obtained by mail from PAIA Electronics, Oklahoma City 73144.)

With the CANCEL switch closed, only the rotating effect is turned off; the unit should still pass the signal at the same relative level as when the effect was on.

The jack on the rear of the case marked SPEED accepts an external 0—9V control voltage and sets the speed of the effect proportional to the positive external voltage. Typical of the devices used to supply this voltage is the PAIA 2730 foot control. Other voltage sources may be used for remote control as long as the positive side of the supply goes to the tip of the jack used to make the connection. When using a remote control voltage, the SPEED control must be turned fully counterclockwise.

The CENTER jack allows remote foot-pedal control of the *center* function. Like the SPEED jack, this input accepts a 0—9V control signal. As the control voltage increases it has the effect of turning the CENTER knob in a clockwise direction. Polarity of the control voltage at the phone jack is the same as for the auxiliary SPEED input, so the same voltage source may be used for either of these functions. When using an external control voltage source the CENTER control should be rotated fully counterclockwise.

Design Analysis. At the heart of the Synthespin is a new integrated circuit package, the LM 3900 quad Norton amplifier. This device consists of four separate differential input amplifier sections, each of which is somewhat similar to the more familiar operational amplifier. It is different in two subtle but very important respects: First, unlike standard opamps, the Norton amplifier is designed as a current differencing rather than a voltage differencing device. Second, the Norton amplifier is meant to work from a single voltage supply rather than the split supply typically used for opamps.

The fact that the inputs of the Norton amplifier are intended as current sinks is implied by the schematic symbol for the device shown in Fig. 2-63. The arrowhead on the noninverting (+) input denotes a current flow into this input, and the circled arrowhead between the inverting (−) and noninverting inputs is meant to imply that there is a constant current sink at this input which is controlled by the signal at the noninverting input.

Because of this current differencing configuration, the Norton amplifier is capable of performing some functions that

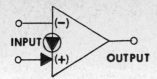

INPUT

OUTPUT

Fig. 2-63. Norton amplifier symbol.

are beyond the capabilities of a standard opamp. Typical of this versatility is the voltage-controlled oscillator composed of amplifiers 1C and 1D. (Note that in schematic diagram the four separate sections of the IC have been labeled as 1A through 1D for clarity.) Experimenters used to working with operational amplifiers will recognize the circuitry surrounding the IC as some sort of strange integrator.

Assume for a moment that Q2 is off. With this condition, there is a current flow into each of the inputs of the amplifier and the amplifier works to make these currents identical. If C12 were not present this would of course be impossible because the value of the resistor at the positive input (R28) is almost half the value of R27 at the inverting input. With C12 in the picture, however, the situation is different; and by constantly and linearly increasing the voltage at its output, the amplifier can cause a current to flow through C12 that, when added to the current through R27, causes the two input currents to be identical. The result is a linearly increasing voltage ramp at the output of stage 1C that would continue to rise almost to the supply voltage if it were not for the Schmitt trigger built around stage 1D.

For the moment disregard C11 and notice that there is positive feedback from the output of stage 1D to the + input. The amplifier compares the two input currents and acts in such a way as to try to make them equal. There is a constant current supply into the inverting input of this amplifier through R31 which is compared to the sum of the current supplied to the noninverting input through R25 and R30. When the circuit is first turned on, the output of stage 1D is at ground (as is the output of stage 1C) so that the current into the noninverting input of stage 1C is very low compared to the current flow through R31. Because of this the output of stage 1D is held low. As the integrator begins to ramp up, the current flow through R25 increases until it exceeds the current flow through R31. At this point stage 1D switches and the output changes from near ground to close to + V_{CC}. The sum of the currents through R25 and R30 now far exceed the current flow through R31 so that the amplifier stays in this high output state.

When the output of stage 1D goes high, it turns on Q2, which now acts as a current sink to prevent any current from being supplied through the noninverting input of stage 1C. The only current now being supplied to the inputs of stage 1C is through the inverting input, so the amplifier must act in such a way as to make this current equal to the current at the noninverting input. The only way it can do this is to constantly and linearly decrease the voltage at its output so that a current flows through C12 that is equal and opposite to the current through R27. This causes the voltage at the output of stage 1C to decrease until at some point the current flow through R31 is greater than the combined current flow through R25 and R30. At this time stage 1D switches back to its low state, thereby turning off Q2 and causing the integrator to begin ramping up again. The result is a triangular wave at the output of stage 1C as it integrates up and down, and a square wave at the output of stage 1D as it switches between its high and low states. The rate at which the voltage rises and falls is a function of the voltage input at point A. The SPEED varies the voltage at this point and therefore the frequency of this oscillator within the limits of 3 Hz, equivalent to over 5 octaves.

Stage 1A in the IC is arranged as a voltage-controlled bandpass filter. R11, R12, C6, C7, C12, and the equivalent impedance of diodes D5 and D6 form a notch filter which is in the negative feedback loop of this amplifier stage. Frequencies outside the notch of this filter pass through the feedback loop with little attenuation and tend to cancel the original input signal of that frequency at the amplifier's input. Signals that are attenuated by the notch are not fed back to the input and therefore do not cancel but are allowed to pass through the amplifier without attenuation. The Q of the active filter is controlled by attenuator R37 in the feedback loop; the time constants of the notch filter section are selected for maximum variability and flattest response over the frequency range from 350 to 1200 Hz. As the voltage across D5 and D6 increases, its equivalent impedance decreases; this causes the center frequency of the notch filter to shift up.

There are three biasing and control voltage sources for diodes D5 and D6. The first, R23 and R24, places the cathode of D6 at about 100 mV above ground. The second is a biasing source consisting of R19, R20, and potentiometer R36. This combination is capable of voltages between 1 and 8V at the wiper of R36. The third supply is the triangle output of the voltage-controlled oscillator, which appears across potentiometer R35. The wiper of R35 picks off a voltage that is a combination of the oscillator output and the voltage at the wiper of R36. When the wiper of R35 is at the end of the pot closest to point C, the voltage from R36 is isolated by the parallel combinations of R35 and R34 and therefore has little effect on the voltage at point B. But as the wiper of R35 is moved away from point C, the contribution of the oscillator becomes progressively less while the influence of the voltage at the wiper of R36 becomes progressively greater. This arrangement allows the voltage at point B to be anywhere between 1 and 8V, with any percentage of that voltage coming from either the oscillator or the constant supply. The voltage at point B is applied to the anode of diode D5 through the low-pass filter section composed of R21, R22, and C8, which converts the triangular output of the control oscillator to roughly a sine wave by filtering out the higher-order harmonic content.

Transistor Q1 provides a means of turning active bandpass filter section 1A on and off. As long as there is no connection between the base of Q1 and ground, it is held on by R15. With Q1's collector at ground, the total biasing current to stage 1A's noninverting input must come from R4.

When the base of Q1 is grounded—as it would be by closing a switch plugged into J3—the voltage at the collector jumps to near $+V_{CC}$, causing C13 to charge through R16. This causes an increased current flow into the noninverting input through R13, and will eventually result in the saturation of stage 1A. With 1A saturated and therefore not functioning, the only element in the signal path is stage 1B, which is arranged for a slight gain into a moderate load at output jack J2.

Part of the original musical input to the circuitry is coupled directly to the stage where it is summed with the output of the bandpass filter. Because of the gains of the bandpass filter and its natural 180° phase shift, the final output is actually a partial cancellation of the signal passed through the bandpass filter and a distortion of phase relationships of frequencies just outside this passband. As the passband sweeps back and forth under the influence of the oscillator, the effect is roughly the same as the frequency shifts generated by a rotating speaker.

In the commercial version, all controllable jacks and knob are accessible from the front panel. Figure 2-64 shows the circuit-board arrangement of these controls.

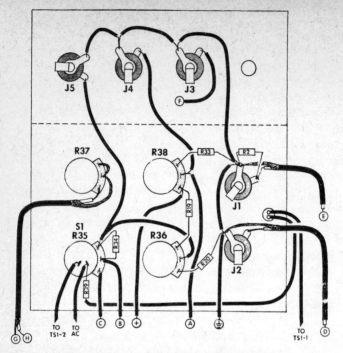

Fig. 2-64. Control layout of Synthespin circuit.

KEYBOARD STORAGE SYSTEM

If you are a novice musician who has at one time or another tried to pick out a tune on an organ, you will know the frustration of trying to beat the metronome. Time is always there to tell you to play the next note at some specific time.

The player piano with its rolls was the answer years ago, but now you can make your own "player rolls" with modern electronic principles. The idea is described briefly here in block diagram form to allow some enterprising individual to pick it up and expand on it.

The basic idea is to store keystroke information. The first step is to encode the information as shown in Fig. 2-65. The switches are a schematic representation of one octave of an ordinary organ keyboard connected to allow the switches to ground the desired inputs.

The STEP/RUN switch and STEP pushbutton allow the system to be operated under the control of a free-running clock (metronome) or a step latch. In the *run* mode the oscillator supplies clock pulses to the address counter. In the *step* mode, the counter is stepped through each count by actuating the STEP pushbutton.

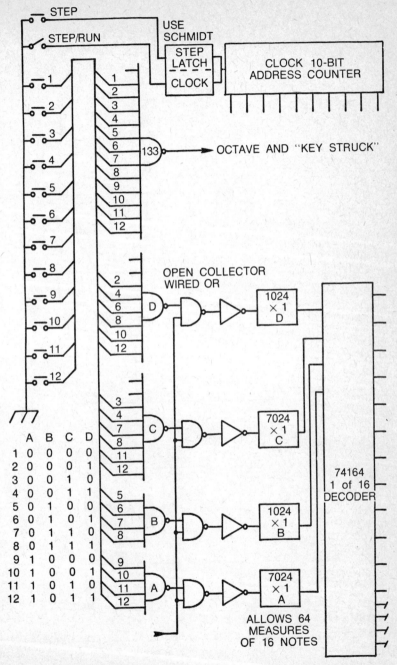

Fig. 2-65. Keyboard storage method. Switches represent keys of organ.

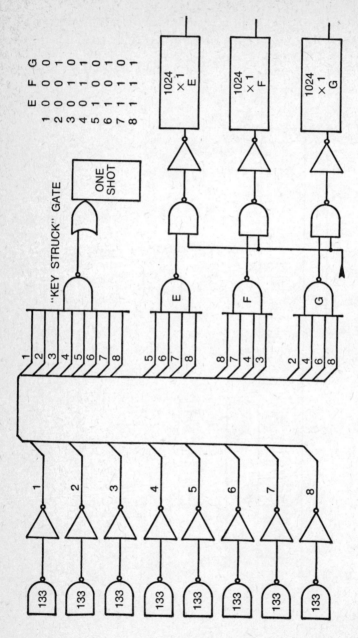

Fig. 2-66. Octave and key struck-logic.

In this way, music can be played at tempo under the control of the clock, or the player can step the unit to the next storage position.

When a key is actuated, it does several things. It grounds one of the inputs (depending on the octave) of the 13 input gates. This "tells" the rest of the logic that a key has been actuated. The inputs of gates A, B, C, and D are also selectively grounded to store a binary number in the addressed location of the 1024-word memory.

The octave and key struck gates (Fig. 2-66) are also gated to store the octave indication in memory sections E, F, and G. The overall result is that a unique number is stored in memory chips A–G, indicating precisely which keys have been struck. This information can now be decoded to actuate oscillators or any other keying system to operate the organ or synthesizer circuits.

In this way, 64 bars of 16th notes can be stored. The user picks out a tune at whatever speed he chooses, getting the chords precisely as he likes. Once the chord is right, he simply steps to the next address. The information is exactly as the last combination of keys struck. After a complete piece has been played through, the STEP/RUN switch is placed in the RUN position and the tune is played over and over as required.

There are undoubtedly hundreds of additional circuits that could be included in this section, but the circuits that follow are those most likely to find a permanent place in most music synthesizers. They will be shown largely without explanation for the builder and experimenter. No great effort has been made to suggest the number or type of circuits or interconnections because it is really very much a matter of personal taste and also depends to a large degree on how much time and money you want to spend.

3 | Understanding Audio Synthesis

There has never been a musical instrument that was conceived overnight and released to the world in an immutable state the next day. Each instrument has undergone change and refinement to bring it to its present condition. The same is true of electronic music but the newness of this field coupled with the technology explosion has caused its development to be compressed in time.

Most of the first electronic instruments were little more than exercises in technology, but some were designed to overcome shortcomings in existing instruments. For instance, the piano keyboard is one of the most powerful musical operating systems available; but it has one outstanding drawback in that while it provides the musician easy access to all twelve notes of the equally tempered musical scale, it prohibits him from using the infinity of musical pitches between those dozen notes. By its very nature it eliminates the possibility of an easy glide from one musical pitch to another.

One electronic instrument designed to overcome this weakness was the *martinot*. The martinot is similar to modern organs in that a standard keyboard is used to control an electronic oscillator built around a frequency-determining resonant circuit. The inductor is tapped at points that produce frequencies corresponding to the chromatic scale; a rather straightforward, if somewhat simplistic, approach to electronically generating a musical scale. In addition to the keyboard there is a finger ring attached to a slider that controls another oscillator. When properly adjusted, this second oscillator produces the pitch corresponding to the keyboard key adjacent to the position of the ring. The combination of keyboard and slider allows the musician to glide from one note to another or add vibrato with a simple move of the hand without sacrificing the operating ease of the keyboard.

The ondioline was a contemporary of the martinot but is significant because it was the first electronic musical instrument to use something other than a sine wave as its basic tone. In the ondioline a relaxation oscillator controlled by the keyboard produced a sawtooth wave which in turn activated several frequency dividers. The output of the oscillator and frequency dividers were combined using much the same techniques employed in some modern organs so that the instrument was capable of generating a great variety of sounds. Observers report that a skilled operator could come close to making an ondioline talk.

While the martinot and ondioline were both designed in France, America's contribution to freeing the musician from the restrictions of the keyboard was probably the most outstanding and bizarre. A theremin has no visible means of control at all and is played simply by moving the hand in relation to two metal plates or rods. Inside the instrument are two high-frequency oscillators, one shielded from any external influences and the second arranged so that the plate or rod forms part of the frequency-determining network. The outputs of these two oscillators are combined in such a way that an audible tone that is the difference between the two frequencies is produced. As the performer's hand is brought closer to the sensing antenna the difference in the two frequencies increases and so does the pitch of the tone. A second circuit allows the performer's other hand to determine the volume of the sound produced. Since there are no frets or keys to provide visual or tactile clues to the pitch a theremin will produce, it is a very difficult instrument to play—but loads of fun.

The first equipment that would come close to meeting our current definition of a synthesizer was built by Dr. Harry Olson during the early 1940s. Produced under the auspices of the RCA Laboratories, the RCA Mark I and Mark II synthesizers were something to behold. The Mark I has been disassembled for some time now but the Mark II still exists and is currently being leased to Columbia-Princeton Electronic Music Center; it measures 17 feet high and is valued at anywhere between $250,000 and one and a half million dollars, depending on whom you talk to.

The average performer might be a little disappointed in the Mark II today because even if there were some way to transport it to a gig, he would find when he got there that he couldn't actually perform a number. The Mark II was simply not capable of real-time operation. Each characteristic of the sound the instrument was to produce was laboriously calculated and plotted ahead of time and the result punched into a roll of paper tape. When it came time for the Mark II to do its thing the tape was fed in like a very large, very expensive player piano. And the results were recorded on a multitrack disc. When all the parts of a number had been recorded on the separate tracks of the disc they were re-recorded on another disc from which a master was made.

You might think that about the only thing the Mark I and Mark II did that was of any consequence was add the word synthesizer to our vocabulary, but that's not the case at all. They were significant first of all because they were the first to put it all together as far as electronic music production was concerned. All the oscillators, amplifiers, and filters needed in one place at one time and some means—no matter how cumbersome—of controlling them all. Second, they were the first instruments to utilize white noise sources as part of the instrument.

Don't get the impression that electronic music cannot be produced without a synthesizer; that's not true. Imagine that you are in a laboratory with all sorts of electronic equipment such as oscillators, filters, amplifiers, modulators, tape recorders, etc. You turn on one of the tape recorders and set the oscillator for the pitch you want, twiddle the knobs of the amplifier to shape the loudness contour, and play with the filter knobs to adjust timbre. It only takes about six hands and a couple of minutes but when you're through you've got a whole note recorded on the tape. Repeat the process often enough and you've got a whole string of notes. Of course, the tempo is not right and the notes may not be in the right sequence but you can fix that by snipping the tape apart and editing out all the junk before splicing it back together again to produce the desired melody. Now you go back and do the same thing for bass, rhythm, and all the other parts; about the only thing you can say for this technique is that it should certainly give you a feeling of accomplishment. Considering the complexity of the process even such monstrosities as dogs barking out the tune of *Away in a Manger* can be forgiven—all that knob twiddling has to do something to a person's mind.

In the early 1960s Dr. R. A. Moog began developing and producing a line of electronic music synthesis equipment that revolutionized the field. The feature that made the Moog equipment such a quantum jump in ease of operation sounds almost ridiculously simple, but its implications are so far reaching that it must be stressed; *the key parameters of the processing elements are a function of the sum of several control voltages rather than the position of a knob.*

As an example of the operating ease of voltage control let's see what it does for a relatively simple processing element, an amplifier. As we shall see a little later, one of the things that contributes most to the way an instrument sounds is the manner in which its sound builds up and dies away. When using the classical tape splicing technique these characteristics have to be duplicated manually for every note by turning the volume control of an amplifier. Even though the Mark II allowed for automatic control of the amplifiers, information still had to be punched into its programing tape for each individual note.

With voltage control the job of setting the correct time-varying amplifier gain can be turned over to an automatic electronic function generator circuit that produces a repeatable, preset voltage waveform each time a key is pressed. This voltage is then used to control the amplifier. The musician sets the function generator to reproduce the characteristics of some real or imagined instrument and the electronics will produce that characteristic for each note he plays. If he desires a totally different sound it's simply a matter of resetting a couple of knobs. Summing the control voltages allows the performer to produce more than one effect from a single processing module. If, in the above example, the operator decides to add a low-frequency amplitude modulation (tremolo) to the sound, he needs only to sum a second voltage that is changing at the rate of the desired tremolo into one of the remaining amplifier control inputs. As the control voltage varies up and down so does the gain of the amplifier and the volume of the sound.

THE SOUND OF MUSIC

Anyone can make weird noises on a synthesizer simply by randomly making connections and pushing buttons. It's even fun for the first hour or so, until you begin to think of specific sounds you want to make and can't. If we're going to learn to use a synthesizer rather than just play with it, it's important that we understand what sound is and what makes one sound different from another.

If your knowledge makes the following discussion seem trite, read on anyway. We have to start somewhere and if nothing else you can probably find something to disagree with.

Sound travels as waves—waves of pressure in the air. A vibrating string displaces the air around it and the air molecules that the string moves bump into and move other molecules. All the things that these sound waves can bump into and be reflected from and the effect that this has on the original wave are beyond the scope of our discussion. The only thing relevant to the subject at hand is that if a man is present the pressure of the waves will finally cause a deflection of his eardrum, which in turn will ultimately cause a disturbance in a fluid medium. This excites the auditory nerves that carry the information to the brain.

The thing that vibrates to produce sound doesn't have to be a string. It can be a synthetic or organic membrane as in a drum, a vibrating reed as in the wind instruments, or the lips of the musician as in the brass instruments. Most important to us, it can also be the cone of a loudspeaker.

When a recording of a musical instrument is made a microphone converts the air pressure waves into exactly analogous electrical voltage waves. If you were to graph the vibrations of the air and the "vibrations" of the voltage side by side they would be virtually identical except that one would be measured in volts and the other in dynes per square centimeter. When these voltage variations are replayed through an amplifier and loudspeaker they are converted from electrical back into sound energy. If all the links in the chain have been faithful in their recording and reproducing functions the pressure waves generated by the loudspeaker will be exactly the same as those originally generated by the musical instrument and the two will be indistinguishable.

The thing that an amplifier and loudspeaker works with is not really sound but an electrical analog of sound; and since it is possible to electronically generate any imaginable voltage waveform (difficult in some cases but possible), it seems only logical that at some point sounds should be generated not by physical musical instruments but by *synthesizing* their electronic analog and then converting that to sound.

THE SYNTHESIS WAVEFORM

Synthesizers are special-purpose analog computers. Before integrated circuits made extremely complex digital computers a relatively low-cost and practical reality, analog computers were used extensively to model real-life mechanical systems. Applications ranged from studying the effects of shock absorbers and springs on the suspension of automobiles to the control of military artillery by means of predicting with accuracy the impact point of a shell based on the ballistics of the weapon.

Modern electronic-music synthesizers are analog computers that are modeling not automobiles or guns but sound sources. Every natural sound-producing system can be broken down into several separate elements. Ordinarily, the first element in the chain is an energy source. A violin draws energy from the bowing action of the performer, a guitar from the deforming force that sets the strings into motion, and wind and reed instruments from the element that vibrates in response to the breath of the musician.

The second element is some means of converting the energy of the system into periodic oscillations of a predetermined frequency. In a guitar the elasticity of the strings causes them to vibrate when deformed and released, in a saxophone the reed converts the steady breath of the musician into a series of pulses.

The last element is some means of coupling the oscillations into the air so that they can be heard. In a guitar the function is performed by the body of the instrument; in a piano it is accomplished by the sounding board; and with wind instruments, the horn structure and shape do the job. The individual characteristics of each of these elements interact to determine how the instrument will sound to a listener.

Dynamics

If the energy is added to the system in a single pulse—as in banging a drum or striking the keys of a piano—the instrument is of the percussion family and all such instruments have the common characteristic of sound intensity at its highest level immediately after the striking action. The period during which the sound output of an instrument is building to its maximum is known as *attack*; an almost instantaneous rise to a peak is known as *percussive* attack. In natural percussion instruments, the attack is followed by an immediate *decay* period, during which the instrument dissipates the energy that was added in the striking force. During the decay the sound falls from the peak it reached during attack back down to nothing. The decay period may be of short duration (as with drums) or long (as with pianos); this is a function of the instrument and the musician's individual control of it.

If the energy is added in a continuous flow, the attack and decay may be separated by a sustain interval during which the

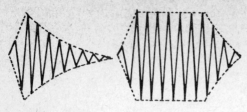

PERCUSSION   SUSTAIN   Fig. 3-1. Typical envelopes.

output of the instrument can be relatively constant. As long as a violinist bows the instrument, sound comes out; as long as the musician's breath holds out he can hold a sustained note with his piccolo.

Figure 3-1 shows an *attack/decay* and an *attack-sustain-decay* envelope. *Envelope* is a term that designates the overall shape of the waveform; it has a considerable effect on the character of the sound despite frequency of the waveform that makes up the envelope. Taken together, attack, sustain, and decay are known as dynamics. These elements make by far the largest contribution to the sound each listener will perceive.

Timbre

All instruments that are capable of sustain intervals don't sound alike—a trumpet doesn't sound anything like a flute—so there are obviously other differences. *Timbre* or *quality* is the term ordinarily used as a label for some of these differences.

The individual timbral characteristics of instruments are the result of two interacting phenomena; first, the waveshape of the oscillations produced by the vibrating element; and second, the resonant characteristics of the coupling device that transfers the energy from the vibrating element to the air.

Not everything vibrates the same way. Figure 3-2 shows four basic examples of raw waveforms produced by the "generators" in natural instruments. The ramp is typical of the situation found in most bowed instruments. In a violin it is caused by the bow grasping a string and deflecting it until the friction of the rosin on the bow is overcome, at which time the string snaps back and is grabbed again. The triangle

RAMP   TRIANGLE   SQUARE   PULSE

Fig. 3-2. Excitation waveforms.

waveform is typical of the back-and-forth oscillatory motion of the body of air within a flute. The square wave is usually produced when one or more reeds alternately open and close to allow bursts of the musician's breath to pass into the instrument. The pulse is often the result of a performer's compressed lips on the mouthpiece of instruments in the brass family. Do not be confused and think that these waveshapes represent the sound of the instrument. These diagrams represent only the way that the vibrating element is behaving; the actual sound results from these waveforms as modified by each instrument's natural resonator.

Figure 3-3 shows a sine wave. A sine wave is sort of a strange beast because there are almost no natural instruments that produce it. It is thought of as a *pure* tone because it has such an insignificant harmonic content. The number, amplitude, frequency, and phase of the various waves required to produce nonsinusoidal complex waveforms are referred to as the harmonic structure of the music. Harmonic structure is a concept that is critical to complete understanding of sound synthesis; but in general, the more gentle the curvature of the waveform, the lower the total harmonic content.

Every physical thing that exists will vibrate when exposed to an energy source. Every physical thing has certain frequencies at which it "likes" to vibrate better than others. The thing—whatever it is—is said to be *resonant* at these frequencies. If the energy applied to the system is periodic (oscillatory) and the frequency of the energy source is the same as one of the resonant frequencies of the thing, then the thing will vibrate more energetically than when the frequency of the energy source is not at one of the resonant points.

The resonant chambers of instruments have certain frequencies that they "like" better than others and tend to filter out the other frequencies. Because of this filtering property, waveforms consisting of various shapes go into one end of an instrument and come out the other with some components of the wave accentuated and others attenuated. Because the amplitude of the components are altered, the

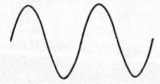

Fig. 3-3. Sine wave.

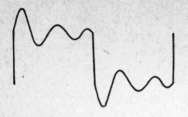

Fig. 3-4. "Ringing" filter response to a square-wave excitation waveform.

overall waveform is altered. Square waves go into one end of a saxophone and a ringing waveform such as the exaggerated version represented in Fig. 3-4 comes out. In stringed instruments the characteristics of the resonant chamber are constant, while in wind and brass instruments the parameters of the resonators must be altered to approximate an equally tempered scale (ETS).

THE MUSICAL ANALOG

Now that we have some idea how the mechanical properties of a musical instrument can affect the sound produced, we will look at how electronic circuits can be used as analogs of those mechanical properties.

Pitched Sound Sources

The electronic analog of vibrating strings, reeds, etc. is the oscillator. Just as the different types of vibrating elements in natural instruments can produce a variety of waveforms, so can the electronic instruments produce a variety of waveforms, so can the electronic oscillators in synthesizers. Most oscillators are capable of producing at least ramp, triangle, and pulse waveforms with the added capability of making the pulse so broad that it becomes a square wave. Many synthesizer oscillators can also produce a sine wave, but just as a pure tone doesn't appear much in natural instruments, a sine wave from a single oscillator isn't particularly important in electronic music.

The pitch of natural instruments is determined by the length of the vibrating string, the pressure on the reeds, or the configuration of the musician's lips and properties of the resonant chamber. In synthesizers the pitch (frequency) of the oscillator may be determined by the magnitude of a control voltage applied to a set of input terminals. Increasing the control voltage raises the pitch of the oscillator. An oscillator controlled by a DC voltage is referred to as a voltage-controlled oscillator, or VCO.

Control voltages can be derived from a number of possible sources including strip controllers, keyboards, programmable sources of various types (sequencers, function generators, etc.) foot pedals and so on. All of these controllers have in common the fact that some action on the part of the musician produces predictable changes in the controller's output voltage.

In the simulation of an instrument's dynamics, synthesizers diverge slightly from their counterpart mechanical systems. It would be natural to assume that the oscillator is keyed or triggered in some way to make its attack and decay simulate the natural instrument equivalent. In fact, the output of the oscillator is constant, and the building up and dying away of the sound is implemented by varying the gain of an amplifier. As you may imagine, it would be at best cumbersome to twiddle the knob of an amplifier fast enough to simulate percussive attack; but voltage control comes to the rescue in the form of the voltage-controlled amplifier (VCA).

In synthesizers, the gain of the amplifier is made proportional to the magnitude of a control voltage, and in most cases this controlling signal is generated by a programmable function generator.

A function generator is simply an electronic circuit which produces a voltage that rises to a preset level in an amount of time set by one control knob (attack) and then falls back to zero in an amount of time set by a second knob (decay). *Sustain* is ordinarily handled by keeping the triggering signal on for the desired interval.

Figure 3-5 shows a typical example of an oscillator feeding a VCA which is being controlled by a function generator to produce the envelope shown.

This leaves us with only one of the most basic natural properties to simulate: timbre. As with mechanical instruments, many of the timbral properties of a sound are the result of the excitation waveform produced by the vibrating element; the remainder are the result of the characteristics of the resonator that couples those vibrations to the transmission medium (the air). Electronic filtering allows us to control a sound's timbral character.

Electronic filters come in a large enough variety that there are engineers who spend the bulk of their professional life designing these single elements. While most of these designs have immediate or potential use in electronic music we will concentrate on the type used in the *Gnome* synthesizer

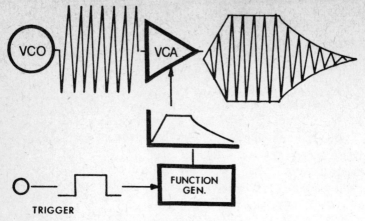

TRIGGER

Fig. 3-5. Using VCA and function

produced by PAIA, since the other circuits we include are fully compatible with this well-engineered system.

Like the natural resonators discussed earlier, bandpass filters have one frequency or band which is allowed to pass through; this passband is called the resonant or center frequency. A sine wave applied to the input of such a bandpass filter will pass through relatively unchanged *if it is at this resonant frequency*; it will be attenuated considerably, however, if it is at some frequency other than resonance. Similarly, the sine-wave components of a complex signal that are within the passband of the filter will be virtually unchanged while the components outside the passband will be attenuated, producing a planned and controlled distortion of the excitation function.

Since many natural instruments count on alterations of their resonators to produce chromatic tones, there must also be some means of controlling at least the resonant frequency of a synthesizer's filter. As you might expect, voltage control is the answer.

Unpitched Sound Sources

To this point we have dealt with pitched sound sources—sources that have a readily discernible repetition frequency and therefore an easily recognized musical pitch. There are also unpitched sources.

The concept of an unpitched musical sound may at first seem as esoteric as the sound of one hand clapping, but it actually requires no meditation to understand. The hiss that you hear from an FM radio that is tuned between stations is an unpitched sound. Most synthesizers have provisions for a noise source that produces just this effect. From a technical standpoint, it is the result of summing together randomly varying amplitudes of all possible frequencies within a given frequency band.

The applications of noise are very broadly based. For example, the sound of the snares of a snare drum may be simulated with a percussive envelope. And by processing noise through the proper filters, the sounds of the surf and the wind are easily simulated, as our earlier circuits have shown.

Now that we have a pretty good idea of why instruments sound the way they do we can begin looking at ways of duplicating these sounds by using electronic circuits.

FREQUENCY AND FORMANT SYNTHESIS

The first method of electronically producing a desired waveform is called *frequency synthesis*. Several oscillators provide a source of sine waves of various harmonically related frequencies, and combinations of the outputs are summed to build up the desired waveform. By changing the amplitudes of the sine waves, practically any waveform can be produced. One of the problems with this system is keeping all of the oscillators tuned so that they are multiples of one another. Most electronic organs that use frequency synthesis systems get around this problem by using one oscillator for the highest frequency component desired and then producing the other frequencies using a chain of frequency dividers.

The technique used in systhesizers is called *formant synthesis* and can be thought of as just the opposite of frequency synthesis. Rather than summing together the frequencies you *do* want, you start off with a source that is already rich in harmonics and then remove the ones you *don't* want. This may seem a rather strange way to get from here to there, but there is an excellent biological precedent for formant synthesis, the most versatile musical instrument of all—the human voice.

If we are going to be consistent in our design of a line of voltage-controlled equipment then everything should be voltage controlled, including the oscillators. Designing a voltage-controlled sine-wave oscillator is not impossible but it is difficult. And hard as it is to design one VCO (voltage-controlled oscillator), designing the five or six that would be required using frequency synthesis, and having them all track the control voltage, would be a horrendous task.

Since synthesizers operate with harmonic-rich waveforms as their primary signal source there is no need to start out with a sine wave at all. Common practice is to use a relaxation oscillator to generate a voltage ramp which is then converted to triangle and pulse waves using simple shaping circuits. In some cases the triangle will also be shaped into a sine wave. These waveforms and their harmonic contents are listed in Table 3-1.

SYNTHESIZER INTERCONNECTIONS AND CONTROL

It is about time that we looked at a problem that has plagued instrument makers since the first caveman beat on a hollow log—how to control the instrument in such a way that you realize its full potential. With most conventional instruments the control system is obvious. You control some of the elements of the dynamics by how hard you blow, pick, or strike the instrument and you control the pitch by the positions of your hands or lips. Timbre is in most cases a quality of the instrument and therefore beyond the control of the performer.

This is not the case with a synthesizer. You have at least the theoretical capability of controlling and varying every characteristic of the sound. Some characteristics you can

Table 3-1. Harmonic Content of Triangle, Ramp, and Square Wave ($\pi = 3.142$ $\pi^2 = 9.872$).

WAVE / HARMONIC	TRIANGLE	RAMP	SQUARE
FUNDAMENTAL	$8/\pi^2$	$2/\pi$	$4/\pi$
2ND	---	$1/\pi$	---
3RD	$8/9\pi^2$	$2/3\pi$	$4/3\pi$
4TH	---	$1/2\pi$	---
5TH	$8/25\pi^2$	$2/5\pi$	$4/5\pi$
6TH	---	$1/3\pi$	---
7TH	$8/49\pi^2$	$2/7\pi$	$4/7\pi$
8TH	---	$1/4\pi$	---
9TH	$8/81\pi^2$	$2/9\pi$	$4/9\pi$

preset by the position of a knob and some you can turn over to automatic function generating equipment. Some parameters are varied with a manual controller such as a keyboard and some, unfortunately, you wind up forgetting about because there are no more controllers available.

Before examining some of the types of controllers that are available, make sure that you have firmly implanted in your mind that a controller for a synthesizer does only one thing: it provides a voltage proportional to some parameter that is physically changed by the performer. While in most cases the voltage produced by the controller will subsequently be used to set the pitch of a VCO, this will not always be the case.

Depending on the sound being produced, the controller may also be used to set the center frequency of a bandpass filter, determine the rolloff rate of a low-pass filter, or any of a number of other things.

Keyboards

When used to control a piano, a keyboard is one of the great inventions of all time. When used with a synthesizer it is at best a compromise.

Musicians are accustomed to keyboards being connected to polytonic instruments; that is, instruments that are capable of playing as many notes at one time as the number of keys that the performer is able to press down. This simply isn't the case with a synthesizer. A synthesizer is a monotonic instrument capable of playing only one note at a time. The reason for this is obvious: The VCO may accept three control voltages, but the pitch that is produced is proportional to the sum of those voltages. Since it is impossible that there be more than one sum at one time, the oscillator can produce only one pitch. By using a rather clever switching system, one brand of synthesis equipment is able to produce two different notes simultaneously but this really not such a great improvement.

Since the electronic organ has become commonplace, performers have gotten used to the idea that they can't control the dynamics of their instrument by varying the striking force on the keys, this is also true of most synthesizers. Other than triggering signals that are generated when any key is pressed, the only control voltage that most keyboards produce is proportional to the location of the key being activated. One manufacturer has a keyboard that is an exception to this rule; in addition to the standard control voltage, it also generates two voltages proportional to the velocity of the key as it is pressed down and the final pressure on the key as it is held down. This is a significant improvement since it allows the performer to directly influence three musical parameters by pressing a single key.

Strangely enough, the original objection to a keyboard was unavailability of pitches between semitones. This is not a great problem on a synthesizer. Most keyboards provide a *pitch* knob that allows some variation in tuning of the instrument, and many provide for an automatic, variable-rate *glissando* (glide).

In spite of its drawbacks, the standard keyboard has one big thing in its favor—familiarity. It is similar to a thing that the musician already knows how to use and retraining time is therefore reduced.

Linear Controllers

These are electrically and mechanically the simplest of all controllers. Most consist of a long strip of electrically resistive material with a voltage applied to each end. The potential difference between the two ends distributes evenly along the length of the strip so that the voltage between any point and electrical ground is proportional to the position of that point on the strip. When the performer presses on the controller, a conducting metal band makes contact with the resistance element and picks off the voltage present at the point of contact.

Linear controllers are generally not intended as substitutes for keyboards for a number of reasons. First, it is technically difficult to automatically produce a trigger pulse whenever the controller is pressed. This function has to be performed manually with a separate switch that must be closed for each note or run that is to be played. Secondly, using a linear controller for pitch is like playing a fretless instrument such as a violin, it requires a considerable experience to know what pitch is going to be produced at a given location.

These devices come into their own when used in conjunction with a keyboard. In this application they can provide an auxiliary control for some parameter other than pitch, like manually sweeping a filter or controlling the amount of noise mixed into a sound. The control voltages produced by this unit can also be summed into one of the VCO control inputs to produce a manually controlled glissando or vibrato or can be used with a VCA to give manually controlled tremolo.

Foot Pedals

Foot pedals allow you to control additional musical parameters with your feet. They are similar to the expression pedals on electronic organs except that instead of controlling only the volume they can be used to control filters, oscillators, or amplifiers.

Joysticks

The biggest thing going for this type of controller is that it offers the possibility of directly controlling four musical parameters simultaneously. One parameter could be controlled by moving the stick forward and backward, another by moving the stick from side to side, a third control voltage could be generated proportional to vertical motions (along the long axis of the stick), and a fourth proportional to the rotation of the handle. If you like you could even put a switch on top to control such vital functions as self-destruct.

A joystick seems like a valid concept, but anyone who could use one properly probably wouldn't be able to communicate with Earth people.

Function Generators

Function generators are automatic controllers that electronically generate a time-varying voltage as preset by the positions of knobs or sliders. A function generator ordinarily responds to a trigger pulse by generating an electrical waveform that rises to some preset value in a preset time, sustains that level as long as the trigger pulse is present, and then falls back to zero. Some function generators are capable of producing the attack, release, sustain, and decay functions discussed earlier.

The output of the function generator can be used in the same ways any other control voltage source should, but these items find their most common application in controlling dynamics and time-varying timbral qualities of a sound.

A low-frequency oscillator also serves as a control voltage source to provide cyclicly varying voltages for vibrato, tremolo, or filter sweeping.

Sequencers

Sequencers can be thought of as extremely versatile function generators. Instead of the control voltage going up to a preset level and back down again, these devices allow a complete sequence of output voltage to be programed and reproduced on command.

Digital Computers

If you are prone to wild flights of fancy, here is a subject worth your consideration. It seems that whenever any of the literature mentions the use of a digital computer in conjunction with a synthesizer it always comes out as a sophisticated sequencer, a high-technology replacement for a roll of paper tape. What a ridiculous waste of the immense computational capabilities of modern minicomputers! Imagine instead a machine that could "hear" the sound of an instrument, analyze it, and then reproduce that sound for any melody the performer chose to play. If you have a touch of larceny in your soul, how about a machine that could hear a person's voice and then duplicate his exact tones for any spoken phrases, or a machine programed with compositional algorithms that could compose tunes to fit your mood. The list is endless.

Patch Cords

In the early days of synthesizers each element of a system was a free-standing module and specific connections were set up using patch cords. Patch cords allow great flexibility but the laborious task of setting up patches for each synthesizer voice is a disadvantage to most performing musicians. In a small system which will not be expanded beyond a specific capability, a normalized connection (one in which a specific

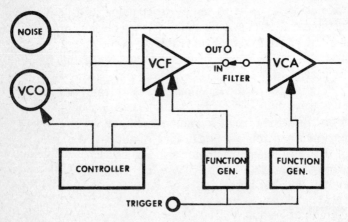

Fig. 3-6. **Gnome** normalization block diagram.

arrangement of elements is prewired) is definitely the way to go.

Gnome Synthesizer Control Elements

Figure 3-6 shows the signal and control paths through PAIA's *Gnome* synthesizer. The VCO always feeds the input of the VCF, and the VCA can get its input either directly from the VCO or from the output of the VCF. The control voltage for the VCA always comes from the function generator dedicated to this element. The control voltage for the VCO can come either from the self-contained controller or the power supply, and is adjustable with the *VCO* RANGE control. VCF control voltages can come either from this element's function generator or the controller, or both. This is a fairly typical normalization scheme for small synthesizers and, while it unquestionably limits the versatility of the machine, the limitations are minimal and entirely consistent with the inherent limitations of the simplified, low-cost circuitry.

The front panel graphics of the Gnome are broken down into six sections corresponding to the six major circuit elements that make up the unit: controller, trigger, noise source, voltage-controlled oscillator, voltage-controlled filter, and voltage-controlled amplifier. The general block diagram of Fig. 3-7 shows the interrelationship of these basic elements.

Controller. The built-in ribbon controller (Fig. 3-8) is nothing more than an exposed resistance element that has its left end grounded and a positive voltage applied to the right end. The sawtooth on the resistance strip along with the paralleling resistors inside the case combine to produce a voltage distribution along the controller strip that is exponential and approximately chromatic. If it were not for this exponential voltage distribution at the controller, semitone intervals at the top end of the strip would seem to be bunched together while those at the low end of the strip would be spread apart. This relates back to the distribution of semitone ETS intervals. Controller strips are available from PAIA Electronics, Box 14359, Oklahoma City 73114. Order part SP-3740-CS.

Range. The controller RANGE potentiometer varies the voltage that appears across the controller strip (Fig. 3-9). At the maximum position of this control the strip is a little less than 4 octaves long while at the minimum setting it is slightly more than ½ octave long. The *controller* and *VCO* RANGE controls interact to place the musical "length" of the

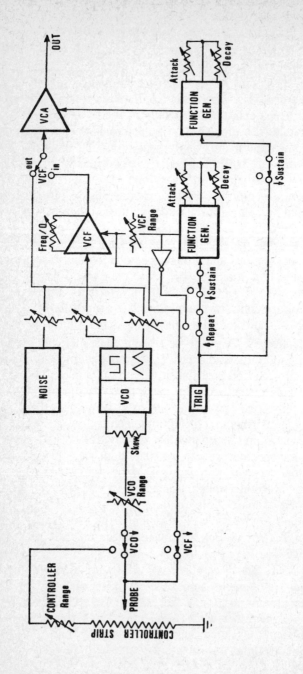

Fig. 3-7. **Gnome** block diagram.

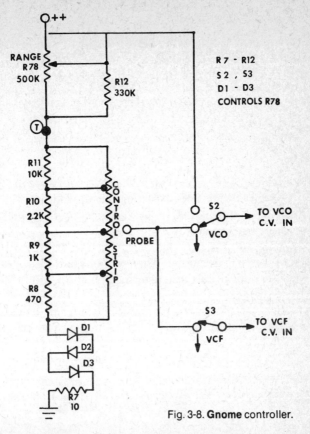

Fig. 3-8. **Gnome** controller.

controller at any desired position within the oscillator's
8-octave range.

VCO and VCF Switches. The two slide switches within the
controller box allow the voltage picked off the controller strip
by the wiper probe to be routed either to the VCO or VCF or both.
Sliding the switch in the direction of the arrow routes the
voltage to the element indicated.

The sawtooth geometry of the conductive elastomer that
forms the controller strip combines with paralleling resistors

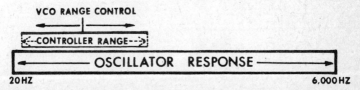

Fig. 3-9. Representation of controller operation.

R8 through R11 to produce an exponential voltage distribution along the surface of the strip.

Controller range potentiometer R78 is in series with the effective resistance of the controller strip, forming a voltage divider. Increasing the resistance of R78 decreases the voltage that appears across the length of the strip.

The wiper probe, which is decoupled by an emitter follower in the VCO to prevent loading of the controller, picks a voltage from the strip that is proportional to the position of the probe along the length of the strip. Switches S2 and S3 allow this voltage to be routed to either the VCO, VCF, or both simultaneously.

The diodes at the bottom end of the controller strip provide a constant voltage drop of approximately 1.5V to insure that there will be sufficient voltage on the strip to drive the VCO regardless of the setting of R78.

Trigger. There is only one control in the trigger circuit (Fig. 3-10): the trigger button. Whenever this button is pressed a voltage is applied to the triggering inputs of the function generators associated with the VCF and VCA. Provisions have been made internally to reduce multiple triggering caused by noisy switch contacts, but a firm pressure on the button is needed to prevent contact bounce.

The TRIGGER pushbutton connects the +18V line to the trigger bus through R1.

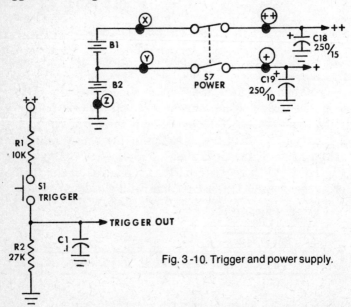

Fig. 3-10. Trigger and power supply.

Noise Source. The single control in the noise circuit (Fig. 3-11) is a level control that determines the amount of white noise that will appear on the common audio bus. At the minimum position of this control the noise source is isolated from the bus; the noise level increases with clockwise rotation.

The noise source is a standard design employing the shot noise that results from the avalanching process of the reverse biased base—emitter junction of transistor Q1. The noise appears across resistor R3 and is coupled by capacitor C2 to the single-stage amplifier comprised of Q2, R4, R5, and R6. R77 is the level control for the noise source; as the wiper of this control is moved toward the collector of Q2, the amount of noise introduced into the common audio bus is increased.

VCO. The VCO of the Gnome synthesizer (Fig. 3-12) contains several specialized controls. The RANGE control is an attenuator on the control voltage input line of the oscillator and is useful in a number of different ways. When the *controller* VCO switch is off, a constant voltage is applied to the *VCO* RANGE control, which allows the oscillator to be set to some constant pitch that is independent of the controller action. When the *controller* VCO switch is on, the *VCO* RANGE and *controller* RANGE controls can be used together to set the highest and lowest pitches available from the strip controller. Figure 3-9 illustrates this by using a bar to represent the total 8-octave range of the oscillator. The double-ended arrow above the bar represents the range of the strip controller. Moving the control increases the length of the double-ended arrow across the width of the bar. For example, with both controls set to

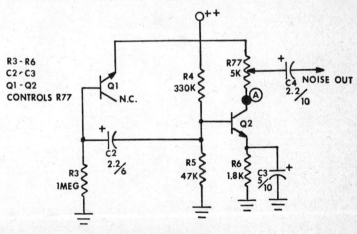

Fig. 3-11. **Gnome** noise source.

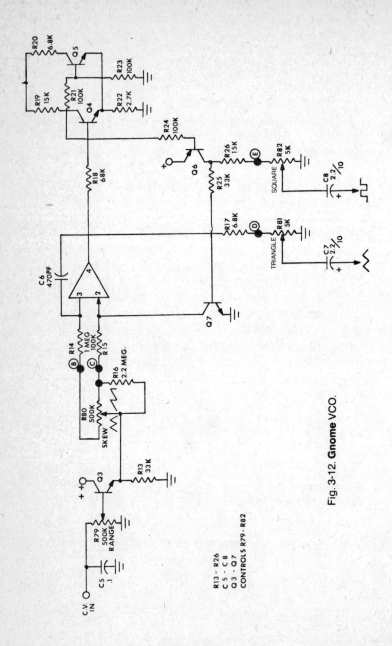

Fig. 3-12. **Gnome** VCO.

R13 - R26
C 5 - C 8
Q3 - Q7
CONTROLS R79 - R82

118

maximum, the range of the controller is approximately from 600 to 6500 Hz. If *controller* RANGE is left at maximum, the controller will remain a little over three octaves long; but reducing *VCO* RANGE can cause these three octaves to run from 30 to 350 Hz. *Note*: The same slight nonlinearities that in most circumstances make the Gnome oscillator incompatible with keyboards will also make the "length" of the controller strip variable, depending on the setting of *VCO* RANGE. Under normal circumstances these errors will not be noticeable or objectionable. At the minimum setting of this control the oscillator is turned off regardless of the condition of the controller or the setting of the *controller* VCO switch.

The SKEW control is a little unusual for synthesizers, but it allows the Gnome's simple VCO to produce the four basic waveforms (triangle, ramp, square, and pulse) while also making available a wide range of combination waveforms. Figure 3-13 shows the effect of this control. Clockwise rotation changes the ramp to a triangle wave and the narrow pulse to a square wave. There is some shift in oscillator pitch associated with the rotation of the control from one end of its travel to the other. This deviation is maximum toward the center of the range of the control with the two extreme ends being within a semitone of the same pitch.

The setting of the control labeled TRIANGLE (Fig. 3-12) determines the amount of ramp/triangle waveform applied to the common audio bus. Level increases with clockwise rotation of the control. The setting of the control labeled

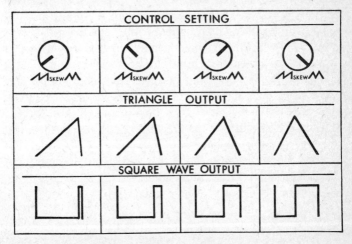

Fig. 3-13. VCO skew control operation.

SQUARE determines the amount of pulse/square waveform applied to the common audio bus.

Control voltages are applied to the oscillator at the point where C5 bypasses contact noise originating at the controller strip. The control voltage is then applied to the VCO RANGE control (R79) which serves as an attenuator on the control voltage line. The wiper of R79 connects to the base of emitter follower Q3, which serves as an impedance matching device between the control voltage input and the oscillator circuitry.

The oscillator is a relatively common type consisting of an integrator built up from one amplifier section of the LM3900 IC and a Schmitt trigger comprising discrete transistors Q4 and Q5 and associated components.

The configuration of the integrator is such that the amplifier will work to make identical currents flow into its inverting (pin 3) and noninverting (pin 2) inputs. Because of the values of resistors R14, R15, and R80, the current into the noninverting input will always be at least twice the current into the inverting input, except when transistor Q7 is turned on. To make up for this difference in current, the output voltage of the amplifier rises linearly to force current through capacitor C6 into the inverting input.

At some point the integrator output voltage exceeds the threshold established by the Schmitt trigger, causing the collector voltage of Q4 to switch from essentially +18V to approximately 3V. Under these conditions, the base–emitter junction of Q6 is forward-biased, causing the collector of this transistor to rise to approximately 9V. The resulting current flow through R25 into the base of Q7 switches this transistor, which in turn effectively shunts the current that was previously flowing into the noninverting input of the integrator to ground. The integrator's amplifier now tries to make up for the surplus current flow into the inverting input by linearly decreasing its output voltage to pull current out of this input through C6.

When the amplifier's output voltage falls to the level at which the Schmitt trigger resets, the collector voltage of Q4 goes high again, which turns off Q6 and Q7 and restores the current flow into the integrator's noninverting input so that the cycle can start over.

The cycle is identical when the SKEW control is rotated toward the ramp position except that the decreased resistance in the noninverting input circuit allows a greater current flow, which causes the integrator's output ramp to rise more quickly. Simultaneously, the resistance taken away from the noninverting input circuit is added to the inverting input to cause the integrator's output to fall more slowly.

The combination of increasing rise time with decreasing fall time keeps the total period of the waveform approximately constant.

The ramping output of the integrator is applied to the series string of R17 and R81, with the setting of the wiper of R81 determining the amount of triangle/ramp waveform that is applied to the audio bus. Similarly, R82 is in the collector circuit of switching transistor Q6; the wiper of this control sets the amount of square/pulse wave applied to the audio bus.

VCF. The VCF circuit with its envelope shaper is shown in Fig. 3-14. All but one of the controls in the VCF are directly related to the operation of the filter's function generator. There are four possible combinations of settings of the REPEAT and SUSTAIN switches, and each combination produces a different response. These combinations are explained in tabular form as in Fig. 3-15.

The RANGE control within the VCF unit is an attenuator on the output of the function generator; it varies the amount of control voltage applied to the filter from the *function generator only*. Since the response of the filters will vary from one unit to the next, this control is designed so that clockwise rotation provides a control voltage greater than the maximum range of the filter. This assures that maximum range will be available on all units.

The ATTACK control determines the time required for the filter's function generator output to rise to its peak. Range of this control is from 5 msec to a little over 1 second.

The DECAY control determines the time required for the output of the filter's function generator to fall from the attack peak back down to no output. Range of this control is the same as ATTACK.

The FREQ/Q control makes changes to the filter itself. Clockwise rotation raises the frequency of the filter while simultaneously decreasing the Q and increasing the loss of the filter. It is normal for the audio to decrease as the FREQ/Q control is turned clockwise.

The VCF is a common design built around one amplifier section of the LM3900; it is tuned by varying the effective resistance of field effect transistor Q8.

The three signals applied to the audio bus are mixed by R34, R35, and applied to the input of the filter through R27.

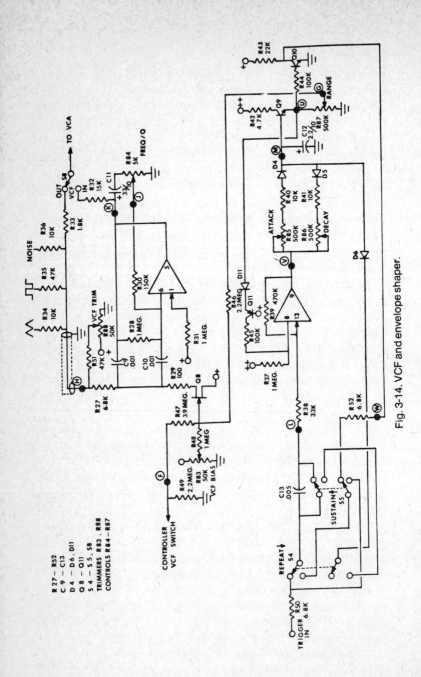

Fig. 3-14. VCF and envelope shaper.

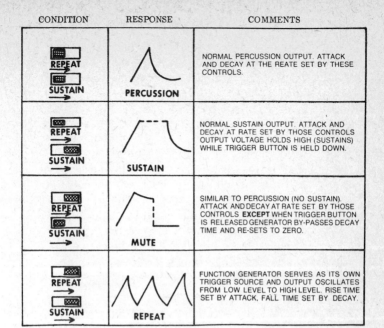

Fig. 3-15. VCF function generator responses.

Slide switch S8 allows either the filtered or unfiltered audio bus signal to be applied to the VCA.

Control voltage for the filter can originate either at the controller strip or at the filter's function generator. Controller voltages appear across R49 and are applied to the gate of the FET through R47, while voltages from the function generator are applied through R46.

The function generator is comprised of one section of the LM3900. Trigger voltages that appear at R38 produce a current flow into the amplifier's noninverting input that cause its output to switch to a high level. This high output voltage causes timing capacitor C12 to charge through R40, the ATTACK control (R85), and forward-biased diode D4. The voltage across C12 is sensed by high-impedance emitter follower Q9, with the voltage at the emitter of this transistor being a diode drop less than the voltage across the capacitor.

Once the amplifier is turned on by a trigger, it is held on by feedback current through R39 even if the trigger is removed. As long as the voltage at the emitter of Q9 is low, Q11 is off and there is no current flow through R45 into the inverting input of the amplifier. As soon as the voltage at the emitter of Q9 exceeds two diode drops (D11 and the base—emitter junction of Q11) above the +9V reference at the base of Q11, this transistor starts to conduct, causing current flow through R45 into the amplifier's inverting input. If the triggering signal has been removed by this time, the amplifier's output resets to a low voltage, causing the charge on C12 to drain off through R41, DECAY control R86, and D5 (which is forward-biased under these conditions). If the triggering signal is still present, it provides enough current into the amplifier's noninverting input to hold the output high for a sustain interval.

Slide switch S5 provides for either sustained or nonsustained outputs from the function generator by allowing either a direct or capacitively coupled input for the trigger signal. Slide switch S4 provides for a repeat function by allowing the normal trigger signal from the TRIGGER pushbutton to be replaced by the collector voltage of Q10. Q10 is a simple inverter stage which produces a high output voltage when the output of the function generator approaches its lowest output.

D6 provides a discharge path from C12 back into the triggering network when a "mute" function is desired from the function generator.

VCA. The voltage-controlled amplifier circuit is shown in Fig. 3-16. Notice the duplication of controls between this unit and the VCF. The SUSTAIN switch within the VCA serves roughly the same function as does the like switch in the VCF. With the sustain off (switch to the left), pressing the trigger button will cause the VCA's function generator to attack and immediately decay. As long as the trigger button is held down the attack and decay times will be as set by these controls; when the trigger is released, a muting function takes over that quickly turns the VCA off.

Turning the sustain switch on (to the right) causes the function generator to hold at the peak level as long as the trigger button is held down. Releasing the trigger causes the envelope to decay at the rate set by the DECAY control.

The ATTACK control within the VCA determines the amount of time required for the output of the amplifier to build to a peak. Range of this control is from 2 msec to slightly more than 1 sec. The DECAY control determines the amount of time required for the amplifier to turn off. Range of the control is from 5 msec to slightly more than 1 sec.

The input that feeds through series resistor R74 is an external trigger input. For best operation the trigger voltage applied to this jack should exceed 8V. Trigger voltages greater

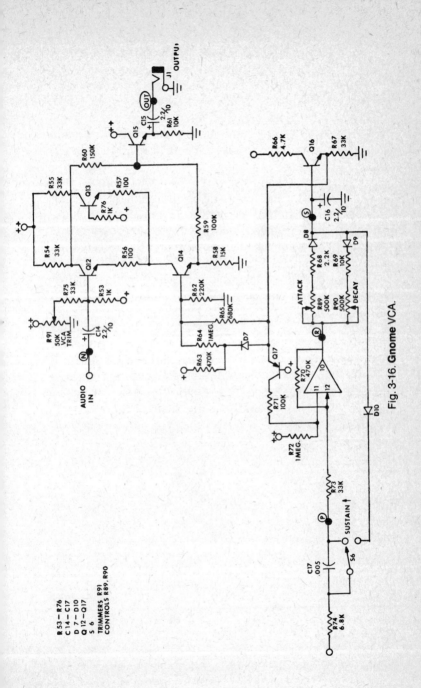

Fig. 3-16. Gnome VCA.

R 53 — R76
C 14 — C17
D 7 — D10
Q 12 — Q17
5 6
TRIMMERS R91
CONTROLS R89, R90

than 4V will produce a triggering action, but if the voltage is less than 8V, the function generator cannot attain its maximum level.

With the deletion of the components that provide for repeat, the operation of the function generator associated with the VCA is identical to that of the VCF function generator.

The VCA is a common design employing a differential pair (Q12 and Q13) sharing a common constant-current sink in their emitter circuits. Since the gain of a transistor is proportional to its collector-to-emitter current, more current flow through the current sink (Q14) increases the gain of the transistors in the differential stage.

In more expensive VCA stages the differential outputs from the collectors of Q12 and Q13 would be applied to the inverting and noninverting inputs of an operational amplifier so that the DC voltage level changes associated with increasing and decreasing the gain of the pair would be rejected as common-mode voltage. In this circuit the DC voltage shifts are canceled out in R59 and R60; this is based on the fact that as the voltage at the collector of Q12 drops with increased gain, the voltage at the emitter of Q14 rises by a proportional amount because of current flow through R58. The ratio of R59 to R60 cancels the DC level shifts while acting only as an attenuator on the audio signal present at the collector of Q12.

Emitter follower Q15 provides a high input impedance to the output of the VCA while presenting a desirable low output impedance to drive the power amplifier being used.

4 | Operational Patching and Setup

In early synthesizers, patch cords were used for interconnecting the various elements to produce the effect desired. The charts that early electronic musicians used to keep records of interconnections were known as patch charts or simply patches. Like most slang, the term remains even though in many cases the patch cords have gone. The settings of knobs and switches that cause a synthesizer to produce a specific effect are still referred to as patches.

VOICING

In the illustrations presented in this chapter, panel likenesses of PAIA's Gnome synthesizer are shown. The various circuits shown in the preceding chapter are described by the panel nomenclature. Settings of knobs and controls are shown by a line extending from the center of the knob to its perimeter (representing the pointer of the knob). An asterisk (*) on any control means that there is special information on the setting of the control contained in the text that accompanies each illustrated patch.

It would be impossible to list all of the possible patches for the Gnome because almost every possible setting of the switches and controls produces some unique sort of sound. These patches that have been selected are simply the starting points for whatever journeys your imagination can conceive.

Whistler

The whistler is simply the triangle-wave output of the VCO being turned on and off by the VCA. In order to achieve manual control, the *controller* VCO switch is turned on so that voltages picked off of the controller strip by the wiper probe are routed to the oscillator. The *controller* RANGE and *VCO* RANGE controls are both set to maximum to achieve the highest possible pitch. The triangle output of the oscillator is selected by turning the *VCO* SKEW control to the triangle designator and turning the triangle output control to maximum. (See Fig. 4-1.) The

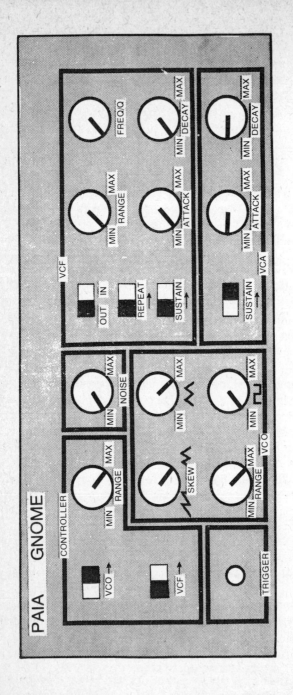

Fig. 4-1. Whistler.

pulse/square wave output is not used in this voice, so the square wave level control is set to minimum.

The filter is not being used, so all of its controls are set fully counterclockwise or off. As a general rule, *any* section of the synthesizer that is not being used should be disabled to prevent any possible interactions between used and unused elements.

The VCA SUSTAIN switch is turned on so that a sound will be produced as long as the trigger button is held down; ATTACK and DECAY controls are set slightly above minimum.

As a variation, substitute square wave, pulse, or ramp for triangle. Juggle VCA ATTACK and DECAY for different effects. Change pitch range by setting *controller* RANGE to minimum.

Dyna-Mute

Dyna-Mute voice automatically sweeps the center frequency of the filter up and down over a harmonic-rich pulse excitation waveform.

Select a narrow pulse excitation waveform by turning the VCO SKEW control toward the ramp symbol and bringing up the level on the square wave output (Fig. 4-2). This time the *controller* RANGE is reduced to restrict the upper frequency of the oscillator. The pitch range of the controller strip is set to include the lowest possible frequencies by pressing the TRIGGER button (VCA SUSTAIN on) while holding the wiper probe down on the extreme left end of the strip. The VCO RANGE control is then rotated counterclockwise until it starts again (should be about 20 to 30 Hz).

The VCF is used this time, so the *controller* VCF switch is set to its right-hand position. And since we are using the VCF's function generator as a control voltage source, the VCF RANGE control is advanced (start with maximum setting and work back as desired). The FREQ/Q is left at the minimum limit of its rotation for minimum loss through the filter. The ATTACK and DECAY controls are advanced just slightly.

The VCA SUSTAIN is turned on so that sound will be produced as long as the TRIGGER button is held down and VCA ATTACK and DECAY are both set to minimum. Pressing the TRIGGER button while selecting a note with the wiper probe will now produce the wah-wah sound so familiar to electronic music buffs.

Wind

The sound of the wind is simulated by sweeping the bandpass filter over the output of a noise source. This patch

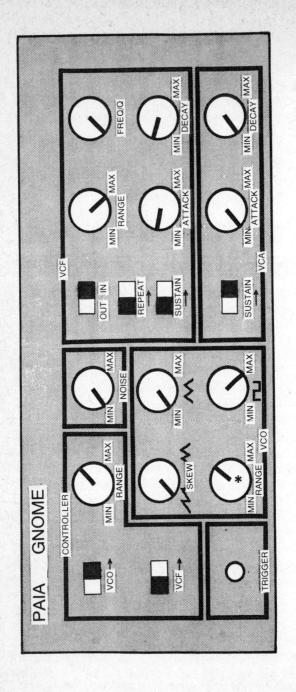

Fig. 4-2. Dyna-Mute.

does not use the VCO, so its controls are all turned down as shown in Fig. 4-3. Instead of setting the pitch of the oscillator the strip controller is now going to vary the center frequency of the filter, so the *controller* VCF switch goes on while the *controller* VCO switch goes off.

Pressing the TRIGGER button while moving the wiper probe up and down over the controller strip will now produce the whistle of the wind.

You may notice that the upper portion of the controller strip produces no discernible change in the sound; if so, it is an indication that the control voltage is exceeding the range of the filter. Press the TRIGGER button and, with the wiper probe held down on the far right end of the controller strip, reduce the controller RANGE control until you hear a slight change in the pitch of the noise. This procedure sets the output of the controller strip to correspond with the control voltage range of the filter.

You may also notice that the noise is not smooth but has some slight popping in the background. This is an indication that the noise source is overloading the filter input; this condition can be cured by turning down the NOISE control.

Snare Drum

The snare drum patch mixes noise (to simulate snare sounds) with a low-frequency triangle (to simulate strike tone), with VCA settings to produce percussive envelope. As shown in Fig. 4-4, the *controller* is not used in this voice at all.

The VCO will be used but its control voltage source will be the internal reference. Turning the *controller* VCO switch off automatically switches in this reference and the pitch of the oscillator can now be set by the VCO RANGE control. While pressing the TRIGGER button bring up the level of the noise source until it sounds like the proper proportion of *snare* sound to *strike* tone.

As a variation, turn *controller* VCO switch on so that the oscillator is controlled by the wiper probe and use *controller* RANGE and *VCO* RANGE to set a control range that is very heavy on the low-pitched end. The result is a chromatic snare drum that you can play tunes on.

Electronic Saxophone

The Gnome is not sufficiently sophisticated to realistically duplicate the sound of many natural instruments, but this

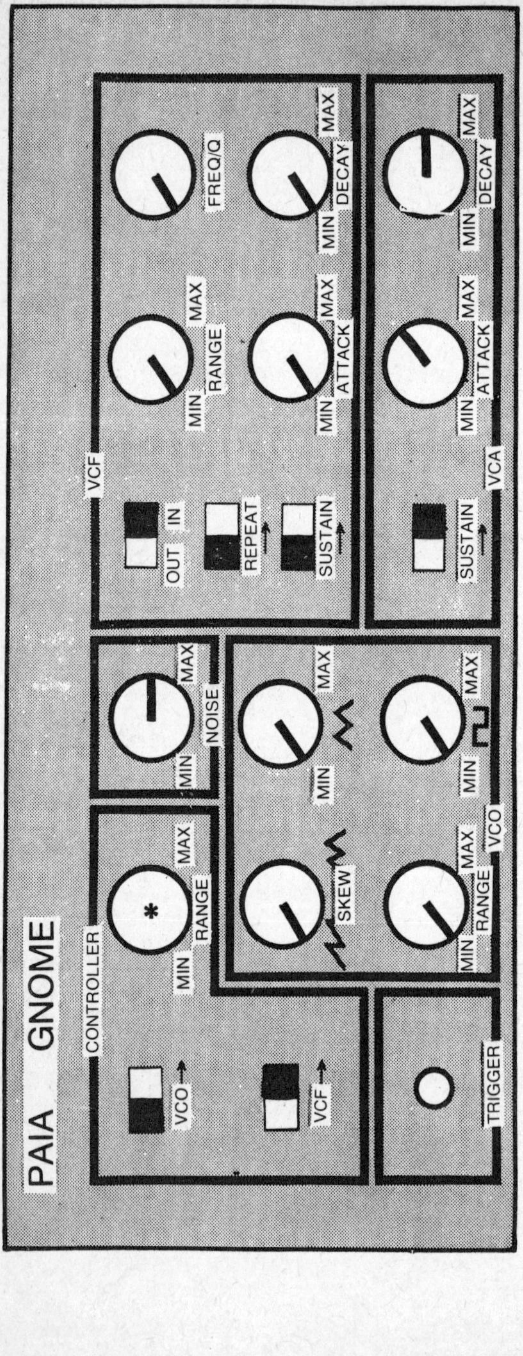
PAIA GNOME
CONTROLLER
MIN RANGE MAX
VCO
VCF
TRIGGER
MIN NOISE MAX
MIN SKEW MAX
MIN RANGE MAX
VCO
MIN MAX
VCF
MIN RANGE MAX
FREQ/Q
MIN ATTACK MAX
MIN DECAY MAX
OUT IN
REPEAT
SUSTAIN
VCA
MIN ATTACK MAX
MIN DECAY MAX
SUSTAIN

Fig. 4-3. Wind.

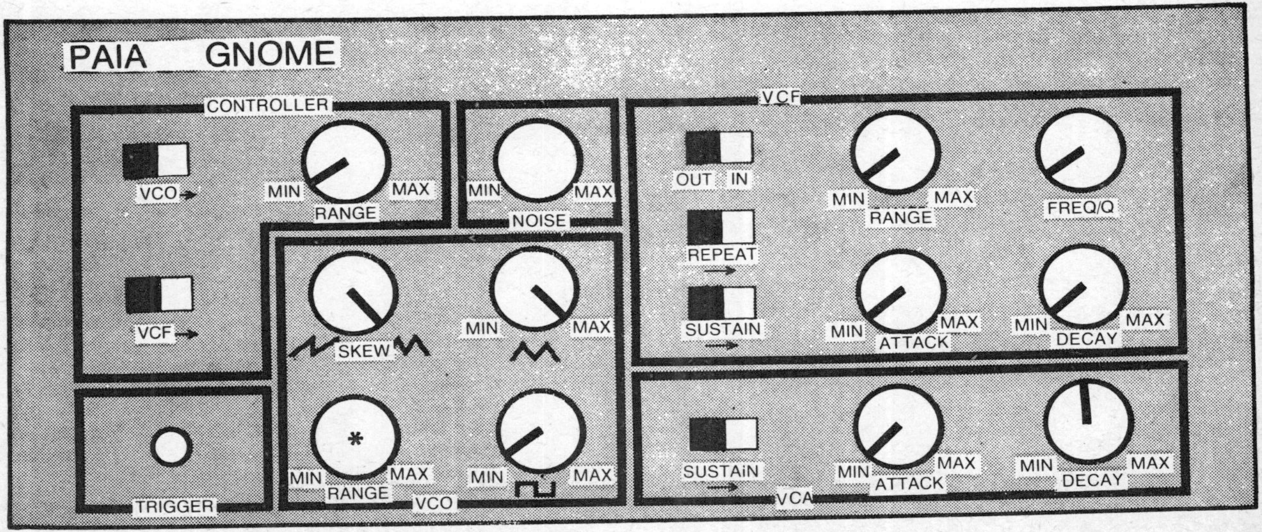

Fig. 3-4 . Snare drum.

patch is roughly the equivalent of a saxophone. It is not intended to sound precisely like the natural equivalent.

In this patch we control both the VCO and VCF from the strip controller. Begin with controller VCF and VCO switches both on and RANGE set to maximum, as shown in Fig. 4-5.

Temporarily bring the NOISE control up and set the controller RANGE as outlined for *wind*. Press the TRIGGER button and slide the wiper probe over the controller strip to change pitch.

There are no natural instruments that have a reverse percussion envelope which builds up slowly and then suddenly stops, but we are used to hearing this sort of sound when it is produced by playing a tape recording backwards. This type of effect can be simulated by sliding the VCA SUSTAIN to off, ATTACK to maximum, and DECAY to minimum.

Summary

The Gnome instrumentation will produce some sort of sound for almost every setting of the front panel controls, with the following provisos.

- The power switch must be turned on (and that's not as funny as it sounds).

- On of the three sound source controls (NOISE VCF TRIANGLE/RAMP level or SQUARE/PULSE level) must be advanced.

- If the VCO is being used, the *VCO* RANGE control must be advanced at least slightly.

- If the *controller* VCO switch is on, the wiper probe must be contacting the controller strip.

- The TRIGGER button must be pressed to produce a sound.

TESTING AND CALIBRATION

There are only three *internal* adjustments: *balance* on the VCA, *bias* on the VCF, and *trim* on the VCF. The rest of this procedure is involved with testing the various sections of the synthesizer to verify proper operation.

Connect a pair of heavy-duty 9V "transistor" batteries to the battery connectors and connect the output line to a suitable amplifier. The auxiliary inputs to most amplifiers are appropriate.

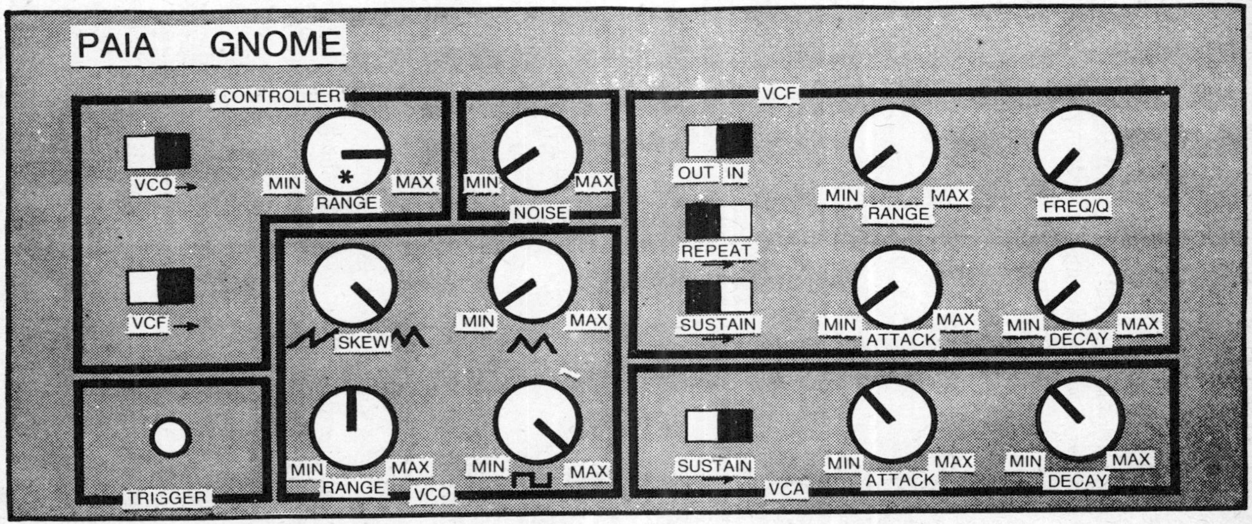

Fig. 4-5. Electronic saxophone.

135

Before beginning calibration, set the controls as follows:

Controller	RANGE min., VCO off, VCF off.
Noise section	Minimum
VCO section	SKEW fully clockwise, RANGE minimum, TRIANGLE minimum, SQUARE WAVE minimum.
VCF section	VCF out, REPEAT off, SUSTAIN off; RANGE, FREQ Q, ATTACK, DECAY, all fully counterclockwise.
VCA section	SUSTAIN off; ATTACK, DECAY minimum.

Turn the external amplifier on and select the proper input channel. Turn the synthesizer on.

Testing the VCA

Rapidly and repeatedly press the TRIGGER button. You should hear a thump from the amplifier that indicates that the VCA is working but needs to be balanced. Again repeatedly press the TRIGGER button while adjusting the VCA *trim* control. At some point in the rotation of the control the thump will be minimum. This is the proper setting for this control.

Testing the Noise Source

Turn the VCA SUSTAIN on and set the NOISE control to maximum (max). Now press the TRIGGER button. You should hear a hissing sound that stays on as long as the button is held down. This indicates that both the noise source and VCA are working properly.

Testing the VCA Function Generator

Rotate the VCA ATTACK and DECAY to max. Press the TRIGGER button. The noise that you hear should take a little more than a second to build up to a peak volume and then remain at that volume as long as the TRIGGER button is held down. Releasing the TRIGGER button should allow the noise to die away slowly, taking a second or so to turn off completely.

Turn the VCA SUSTAIN switch off and once again press the TRIGGER button. Even though the TRIGGER button is held down, the noise should build to a peak and then immediately begin to die away. Press the TRIGGER button and release it before the entire attack and decay cycle is completed. As soon as the TRIGGER button is released the sound should go off. This is an automatic muting function that is operative any time the VCA SUSTAIN switch is off. Successful completion of this sequence of tests shows the VCA function generator to be operating properly.

Testing the VCO

Return the NOISE control to minimum (min) and advance the *VCO* SQUARE WAVE control to max. Return the *VCA* ATTACK and DECAY controls to min. Press and hold the TRIGGER button while advancing the *VCO* RANGE control toward max. During the first 30° or so of rotation of the *VCO* RANGE control you should hear nothing. After about 30° of rotation you should hear a low-pitched tone from the amplifier. As the control is advanced further, the tone should rise in pitch. Return the *VCO* SQUARE WAVE control to min and advance the TRIANGLE control to max. Press and hold the TRIGGER button while once again rotating the *VCO* RANGE control. Once again you should hear a tone that increases in pitch as the *VCO* RANGE control goes from min to max. This tone should be mellower than the square wave but the frequency range should be the same and you should have the same "dead zone" at the counterclockwise end of the rotation of the RANGE control.

Leave the *VCO* RANGE control at some intermediate position so that a steady tone is coming from the amplifier, and rotate the SKEW control in a counterclockwise (CCW) direction from the triangle symbol toward the ramp symbol. The frequency will increase slightly as the SKEW control is rotated, but it should not vary more than a couple of semitones from the pitch at the ends of the rotation.

Notice that with the SKEW control set toward the ramp symbol, the tone is considerably sharper than the triangle wave tone. Take the TRIANGLE control to min and the SQUARE WAVE control to max, and verify that the resultant tone is the sharpest of all. Successful completion of this test sequence verifies the proper operation of the VCO.

Testing the VCF

Return the *VCO* SQUARE WAVE control and RANGE to min. Turn on the VCF and advance the NOISE control to max. Set the *VCF* SUSTAIN switch to on. Set the VCF *bias* trimmer (R83) fully CCW. Rotate the adjusting disc of the VCF *trim* control (R88) fully. Make sure that the *VCF* RANGE control is set to min and press and hold the TRIGGER button. While listening to the noise, rotate the adjusting disc of the VCF *trim* control (R88). You should hear the apparent pitch of the noise increase as the passband of the filter sweeps upward in frequency. Set VCF trim to the point at which the pitch of the noise just begins to increase.

Rotate the VCF RANGE control to max and observe that the pitch of the noise once again increases. Now rotate the adjusting disc of the VCF *bias* trimmer (R83) clockwise (CW), and observe that at some point the pitch of the noise begins to decrease. Leave the VCF *bias* trimmer set at the point at which the pitch of the noise just begins to decrease.

Return the VCF RANGE control to min and once again advance the VCF *trim* control until the point is reached at which the pitch of the noise just begins to increase.

Testing the VCF Function Generator

Set the VCF RANGE control to about half of its rotation and the NOISE control to max. Slide the VCF REPEAT switch on and press and hold the TRIGGER button. This setting of the VCF function generator controls (SUSTAIN on, REPEAT on) causes the function generator to trigger itself, producing a cyclic sweep of the filter. In this case the sound produced should be a swishing as the filter sweeps up and down over the frequency content of the noise. Observe that the depth of this effect increases as the VCF RANGE control is rotated.

At this maximum repetition rate (VCF ATTACK and DECAY both at min) there will probably be some thumping from the synthesizer. This transfer of the control voltage into the audio channel can be eliminated by reducing the setting of the VCF RANGE control or by slowing the attack and decay of the VCF function generator.

Observe that as the FREQ/Q control is rotated in a clockwise direction the overall pitch of the noise increases.

Return the VCF FREQ/Q control to its fully CCW position and RANGE to max. While holding the TRIGGER button down, advance the VCF ATTACK to max and observe that the pitch of the noise slowly builds up to a peak and that this effect occurs cyclicly. Return the VCF ATTACK to min and advance the DECAY to max. Observe that now the pitch of the noise goes to a high value and then slowly slides back down the scale until again it resets to the high level. Set the VCF ATTACK to max and observe that the filter slowly sweeps up and down the scale.

The VCF RANGE control is designed to have greater effect than is actually needed. If, during the last test, the pitch of the noise seems to increase to a plateau and then hold momentarily before sliding back downscale, it indicates that the RANGE control is too far advanced. Back off slightly until the plateau disappears. Successful completion of this test sequence indicates that both the filter and function generator are operating properly.

Set the VCF controls as follows: RANGE max, FREQ/Q min, VCF on, REPEAT off, SUSTAIN off, ATTACK min, DECAY max. Press and hold the TRIGGER button. You should hear the noise apparently starting at a high pitch and decaying back to a low pitch. It should not repeat but rather stay at the low pitch until the TRIGGER button is released and pressed again.

Set ATTACK to max and DECAY to min. Pressing the TRIGGER button should produce noise that increases in pitch over a period of a second or so followed by a rapid step back to low pitch. Once again, this pattern should not repeat until the TRIGGER button is released and pressed again. Set DECAY to max and observe that the pitch of the noise slowly sweeps up and back down each time the TRIGGER button is pressed. Set the *VCA* DECAY control to max, *VCA* DECAY to min, and slide the *VCF* SUSTAIN switch to its *on* position. Press and hold the TRIGGER button. Observe that the pitch of the noise always sweeps up to a high level and remains there until the TRIGGER button is released. Successful completion of these tests indicates that the synthesizer is operating properly.

5 | Synthesizer Design & Operational Considerations

There are 12 semitones in each octave of the chromatic scale: 7 naturals labeled A through G and 5 accidentals that are designated as either sharps or flats of the naturals. With two exceptions, the sharp of one note is identical to the flat of the next highest note; there are no accidentals between B and C or between E and F, so that B-sharp is the same as C and F-flat is the same as E.

For each octave increase in the musical scale the frequency of the note doubles; since middle C corresponds to 261.6 Hz the next C above middle C is 523 Hz.

Somewhere back in antiquity (around the time of J. S. Bach) some genius decided that since there are 12 semitones to the octave and each octave doubles the frequency, each note should be related to the note directly below it in the scale by a factor of the twelfth root of two. Just in case you're not used to working out of the twelfth root of numbers in your head, this translates to 1.059 times the frequency of the note directly below it. The significance of this is that as pitch increases, the *difference* between adjacent notes in the scale also increases.

All this may seem like academic trivia until you realize one point. Voltage-controlled oscillators produce an output frequency that is directly proportional to the control voltage; and identical control voltage changes produce identical frequency changes.

An example will most readily demonstrate the significance of these facts. Suppose that we have a keyboard that produces a control voltage of 0.625V when its lowest C key is pressed. The voltage corresponding to the next C is quite logically 1.25V. But don't fall into the trap of thinking that the voltage corresponding to the third C is 1.875V (1.25 plus 0.625), because it's not; it should be twice the voltage required for the second C or $2 \times 1.25 = 2.5V$.

Many synthesizer designers use an electronic conversion device to get around this difficulty. This device converts a

140

linear controller output voltage (1V for the first C, 2V for the second, 3V for the third C, etc.) to the octavely related voltage required by the VCO. This is an excellent approach if you are willing to spend the money to do it, because it allows two oscillators to be a fixed number of semitones apart and still track a control voltage is such a way they maintain an equally tempered relationship.

Unfortunately, the exponential converter circuits (as these devices are known) are not only expensive but unstable; they tend to drift so that even for a fixed input voltage, the output voltage (and, of course, pitch of the VCO) wanders from one value to another.

A simple means of getting around this is to have the keyboard generate octavely related voltages in the first place; but you of course sacrifice the capability of having two oscillators track each other.

VOLTAGE-CONTROLLED AMPLIFIER

The biggest concern in the design of a voltage-controlled amplifier is that none of the control voltage transfers into the audio channel. If there is leakage between the two, very rapid changes in control voltage (such as the fast attack of percussion waveforms) will become audible as clicks or thumps. The PAIA design (Fig. 5-1) is such that the control voltage appears identically in two separate amplifiers and is then balanced out by an operational amplifier output stage. Nothing special here—this is the way practically all synthesizers do it. The unit depicted differs from many synthesizer modules in the way the control voltages are summed together. In expensive equipment this summation is performed by an active network built around an operational amplifier. In Fig. 5-1 the summing is performed by three resistors.

The advantage of this approach is obviously cost; the disadvantage (in a technical sense) is that the summation is never exact and the voltage applied to one input can have a small influence on the effect of a voltage applied to another input. If the resistors sum into a point that has a low impedance in relation to the summing resistors, this effect is negligible for all practical purposes. One justification for using this slightly less exact summing network is that the human ear is less sensitive to changes in intensity of a sound then any other parameter; even a trained listener couldn't likely tell the difference between active and passive summing networks.

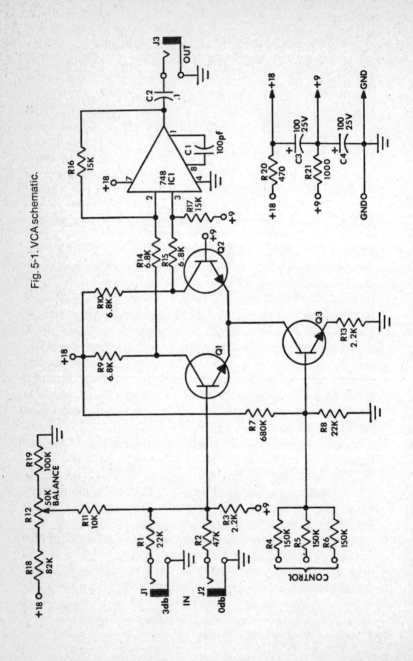

Fig. 5-1. VCA schematic.

142

The design of the amplifier is such that if the voltages at the control input add up to +5V there is zero insertion loss between the 0 dB audio input and the audio output. Voltages less than +5V cause the amplifier to present a greater and greater attenuation to the audio signal until, at a total control input of 0V, the amplifier can be considered *off*. Negative control voltages and voltages greater than +5V will not damage the amplifier, but if the control voltage input goes higher than 6V, distortion will develop.

At the maximum control voltage of +5V there is a 3 dB power gain between J1 and the output. The 3 dB represents a doubling of power. The two input terminals (J1 and J2) have a slight DC potential and must be capacitively coupled to audio sources. All audio sources described in this book already have a capacitive output coupling, but if electrified musical instruments are being processed, this capacitor must be supplied externally.

Design Analysis

The voltage-controlled amplifier provides the synthesist with a versatile means of shaping the amplitude contour of synthesized sound. The gain of the amplifier module is dependent on the sum of the voltages at three control inputs. Two audio input jacks allow the VCA to be used as a mixer/amplifier, and weighting of the audio inputs allows one signal to have a 3 dB boost, as already noted, over the other without using external attenuators. The excellent low-frequency response of the circuit shown permits this module to process not only audio but control voltages under some conditions.

Referring to Fig. 5-1, the three control voltage inputs are summed by resistors R4, R5, and R6, and used to set the amount of current that constant-current source Q3 supplies to the differential pair (Q1 and Q2). The amplification produced by the pair is proportional to their collector currents; as Q3 supplies more current, the gain of the pair increases.

Along with increased gain, the greater current flow also produces a greater quiescent voltage drop across load resistors R9 and R10. When the circuit is properly balanced using trimmer R12, the increase in this voltage is equal while the audio signal applied to the base of Q1 appears inverted at the collector of Q1 and noninverted at the collector of Q2.

Using the balanced input of an opamp, the in-phase collector voltages caused by the gain-setting current can be eliminated while the out-of-phase audio signal is amplified. This eliminates any popping as the amplifier is switched.

Two inputs through summing resistors R1 and R2 allow the amplifier to be used as a mixer; the ratio of these two resistors is such that the input through R1 produces a 3 dB greater output than the input through R2.

Testing

The VCA may be tested using only an audio signal source and amplifier. Connect the power supply to the terminals on the rear edge of the circuit board.

Turn on the amplifier you will be using and temporarily jumper its input to the output of the audio signal source.

If you are using the voltage-controlled oscillator shown later in this chapter, set an audible pitch by using a −5V to +5V bias source as a control input. Adjust the volume of the amplifier for a comfortable listening level. If a signal source other than the VCO is used, set it for about 1000 Hz with a peak-to-peak amplitude of 0.5V.

Disconnect the jumper between the oscillator and amplifier. Jumper the output of the oscillator to the *0 dB* input of the VCA. Make sure that there is DC isolation between the VCA and oscillator. If there is no isolation, put a 0.1 μF ceramic disc or Mylar capacitor in series with the connection between the VCA and oscillator. Jumper the output of the VCA to the input of the amplifier. Apply a 5V bias to one of the control inputs of the VCA and observe that the volume is approximately the same as when the oscillator was feeding the amplifier directly (some adjustment of trimmer resistor R12 may be necessary). Turn off the 5V bias and observe that the tone is turned off.

With the control voltage still at 0V, change the oscillator output from the *0 dB* to the *3 dB* input of the VCA. There should still be no tone. Once again rotate the 5V bias control fully clockwise and note that the tone is slightly louder than when the signal is being applied to the *0 dB* input.

Disconnect the 5V bias supply from the VCA control input jack. Tap the point of the pin plug against the metal contact inside the jack and observe a popping sound from the amplifier. Adjust trimmer R12 to minimize this pop. Because of the electrical noise generated from mechanically making and breaking this connection, there will always be a little popping associated with this test. Unless the pop is severe (regardless of the setting of R12), it will present no problem when the amplifier is driven from any of the electronic control voltage sources.

Test all three of the control voltage input jacks to make sure that a 5V input to each one turns on the amplifier.

The VCA in Practical Operation

There are some design constraints that must be placed on a voltage-controlled amplifier; primary among these constraints is its response to a very rapid increase in control voltage. Most of the time you will be using the VCA to control the amplitude of an audio signal. In order that percussion effects such as drums sound realistic, the amplifier must go from a completely isolating condition to unity gain in about 2 msec. None of this control voltage can be allowed to transfer into the audio channel or there will be ferocious pops and thunks from the speaker. Using a differential input stage with a common constant-current source guarantees that this won't happen.

Control voltage summation is not as important in the VCA as it is in the VCO because the human ear is not particularly sensitive to changes in the amplitude of a sound. Thanks to this, the summation performed on the VCA voltages need not be exact and a simple resistive summing network does the job.

The gain of the amplifier is set by the algebraic summation of the control voltages that are present at the three control jacks. The amplifier is designed so that if the voltages at the control input add up to +5V there is zero insertion loss between the 0 dB audio input and the audio output. Voltages less than +5V cause the amplifier to present a greater attenuation to the audio signal, until at a total control input of 0V the amplifier can be considered off.

The need for algebraic summation of the control voltage can most easily be explained with a simple commonplace example. Assume that you want to process an audio tone so that it has the maximum tremolo (cyclic amplitude variations) possible. Obviously you will use the VCA to vary the amplitude of the tone, the control oscillator to supply the tremolo control signal, and the function generator to give the final sound the attack and decay characteristics you need.

So you route the control oscillator into one of the control inputs on the VCA and crank the tremolo voltage up all the way (+5V peak-to-peak) and out comes the greatest tremolo ever, the sound is going from full on to full off. Now you connect the output of the function generator to one of the remaining two

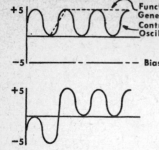

Fig. 5-2. Summation of three control voltages—ramp, sine wave, and constant bias.

control inputs of the VCA—but the sound is still there because the amplifier is already being turned all the way on and off by the control oscillator. Not only that, but when you hit the function generator trigger button, a bunch of distorted mush comes out because at some points the sum of the +5V function generator output and the +5V peak of the control oscillator add up to +10V, way above the permissible control voltage input. You could use two VCA modules—one to process the tremolo effect while the other does the attack and decay—but thanks to algebraic summing there is an easier way. Simply sum a constant −5V bias into the remaining VCA control input.

The overall effect of these summations is shown in Fig. 5-2; but in words, the −5V bias cancels out the +5V peaks of the control oscillator so that the amplifier is off until the function generator is triggered, at which time its +5V output cancels the −5V bias, leaving only the 0−5V signal from the control oscillator to produce maximum tremolo.

VOLTAGE-CONTROLLED OSCILLATOR

The VCO is the one place in a synthesizer that you can't scrimp because, as mentioned earlier, *pitch is the audio parameter to which the human ear is most sensitive*. Control voltage summation has to be exact and oscillator drift must be kept to a minimum.

In order to provide exact control voltage summation, the VCO circuit shown in Fig. 5-3 uses an active summing network built around an IC operational amplifier (opamp). Frequency drift caused caused by voltage variations may be minimized by keeping the two independent voltage regulators on the VCO circuit board.

There is one place that cost was cut in the circuit shown: the omission of a sine-wave output. Several factors entered into the decision to eliminate this common and useful waveform, but in the final analysis they all boiled down to the added cost and space requirements necessary to produce the sine wave as compared to the ease of using the voltage-controlled low-pass filter to derive the sine wave from the triangular wave.

The three input jacks (J4, J5, and J6) accept voltages from keyboard, linear controller, control oscillator, function generator, etc. and set the frequency of the oscillator such that is directly proportional to the algebraic sum of the three imputs. Normal range of the sum of the three inputs is 0—5V but the oscillator circuit shown will track up to 100% overrange. Negative voltages and voltages greater than 5V will not harm the module.

The RAMP output of the VCO (J1) produces a sawtooth waveform that has a very "reedy" sound. The TRIANGLE output (J2) produces a soft sound that is comparable to the voice of a flute. The PULSE output (J3) produces a waveform that is variable between a short pulse and a square wave. This is the "raspiest" sounding of the three waveforms and is an excellent harmonic-rich source for use with voltage-controlled filters.

The PULSE DURATION control knob (located below J1 on the schematic) varies the duty factor of the pulse output. At the minimum setting the output is just a spike; at the other extreme, duty factor is greater than 50%.

Design Analysis

The voltage-controlled oscillator provides ramp, triangular, and variable-duration pulse outputs at a frequency that is directly proportional to the sum of the voltages present at the three input jacks. Control voltage sources can be keyboards, linear controllers, programers, and so forth.

Features of the module include opamp summation of the control voltages, local voltage regulation on the circuit board for maximum oscillator stability, and buffered audio outputs that allow simultaneous use of all three waveforms.

The three control inputs are summed by the opamp summer built around the IC. Trimmer resistor R7 (RANGE) increases or decreases the feedback resistance and consequently the gain of the circuit. Trimmer resistor R4 (ZERO) provides a variable input to the summing circuit and allows the offset (summed voltage out with no control voltage inputs) to be varied.

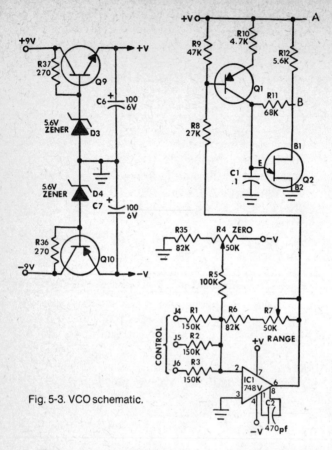

Fig. 5-3. VCO schematic.

The output of the summing circuit is applied to the voltage divider consisting of R8 and R9, which in turn sets the current available from constant-current source Q1. The constant-current source charges C1 which, in conjunction with the unijunction transistor (Q2), forms a relaxation oscillator. As increasing voltages are applied to the control inputs, the current supplied by Q1 increases, causing C1 to charge more rapidly and increasing the frequency of the relaxation oscillator.

The voltage that appears across C1 is a ramp that increases linearly up to the firing threshold of the unijunction transistor and then rapidly drops back as the capacitor discharges through the conducting emitter—base-1 junction of Q2. This voltage ramp is applied to buffer Q3; from there it is used three ways:

First, it is applied to the voltage divider string consisting of R13, R25, R26, and R27. Between R13 and R25 the string is

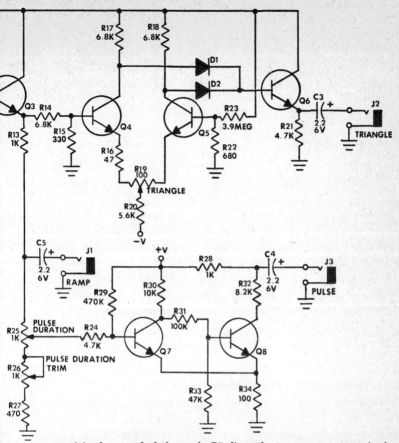

capacitively coupled through C5 directly to RAMP output jack J1 where it becomes available as a signal source.

Second, the ramp is applied to the Schmitt trigger composed of Q7 and Q8. A Schmitt trigger has a low output or a high output depending on whether the input voltage is above or below a preset design level. As the ramp input to the trigger begins to rise, the output remains low until the voltage exceeds this level and then abruptly changes to the high state. The output of the trigger, then, is a rectangular pulse at exactly the frequency of the ramp input. By varying the amplitude of the ramp, the pulse width is regulated to some value as illustrated in Fig. 5-4.

Third, the ramp is applied to the input of the differential pair (Q4 and Q5). In the differential configuration the voltage at the collector of Q5 is in phase with the input ramp and the voltage at the collector of Q4 is inverted. Diodes D1 and D2 select the higher of the two collector voltages and apply it to

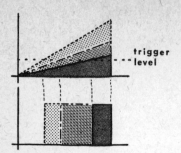

Fig. 5-4. Effect on pulse duration of increasing the amplitude of a ramp input to a Schmitt trigger.

the base of emitter follower Q6. During the lower half of the input ramp's excursion, Q4's collector voltage is higher and that section of the ramp is presented in an inverted form to the base of Q6. During the second half of the ramp, the collector of Q5 is higher and this portion of the ramp is applied to the base of Q6 in a noninverted form. The net result is a triangular wave appearing at the emitter of Q6. There is a slight rounding at the bottom of the wave during the crossover between Q4 and Q5 and a slight pip at the top during the ramp flyback; but neither of these imperfections are audibly noticeable.

Power for the vco is regulated by simple series regulators Q9 and Q10 using the voltage across zener diodes D3 and D4 as references.

The VCO in Practical Operation

Because the human ear is so much more sensitive to changes in pitch than it is to changes in harmonic content, volume or any other audio parameter, there can be little cost cutting in the voltage-controlled oscillator. Things like exact voltage control summation and parameter stability versus temperature and line voltage that are not a problem in the filter or amplifier module must be compensated for in this primary pitch source.

The three input jacks accept control voltages from keyboard, linear controller, control oscillator, function generator, and similar sources and set the frequency of the oscillator such that it is directly proportional to the algebraic sum of the three inputs. Normal range of the sum of the three input voltages is 0−5V, but the oscillator will track up to 100% overrange. That is, a +10V input will cause the frequency of the oscillator to be twice what it was at +5V.

Calibration and Testing

A variety of methods may be used to calibrate the voltage-controlled oscillator. The first method requires the use of considerable test equipment and will result in the fastest possible tuning. In later paragraphs a method is described which requires only a voltohmmeter (VOM) and piano, organ, or other tuned musical pitch reference. The second method produces a very accurate calibration but at a sacrifice in speed.

It is desirable that you understand not only the "how" but also the "why" of the calibration procedure. The purpose of any calibration is to compensate for component tolerances between supposedly identical circuits. Specifically, the calibration of the circuit will do three things:

- Adjust pulse circuitry so that the PULSE DURATION control will have maximum useful range.
- Align the ramp-to-triangle converter so that a near-perfect triangle is available.
- Align the control-voltage summing circuitry so that at a given control-voltage input the oscillator produces a given frequency. This is an elusive thing. Since two interacting adjustments must be made, the procedure you will be using will be one of successive approximations, where certain steps will be repeated, each pass reducing the error.

Before starting on the calibration, apply ±9V power to the VCO. Any suitable bench supply may be used but because of the heavy current drain, batteries are not a suitable supply. Turn the power on and allow 20 to 30 minutes settling time before calibration. Set trimmers R7 (RANGE), R19 (TRIANGLE), and R26 (PULSE TRIM) to the midpoint of their rotation. Set trimmer R4 (ZERO) to the clockwise limit of its rotation. Set PULSE DURATION control to its counterclockwise limit.

Calibration Method 1. You'll need an oscilloscope, audio generator, VOM, and a variable DC supply. Connect the vertical input of the oscilloscope to the RAMP output of the VCO and verify that the peak-to-peak output from this jack is 0.5V (±20%).

Connect the vertical input of the oscilloscope to the PULSE output of the VCO and adjust the sweep rate so that two or three pulses are visible on the scope. Adjust trimmer resistor R26 for the narrowest possible pulse without losing pulse height. Verify that the peak-to-peak amplitude of the pulse is 0.5V and that rotating the PULSE DURATION control varies the duration of the pulse from a narrow spike to about 50% or more duty factor *without changing the overall period*.

151

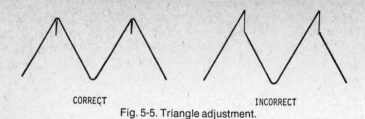

CORRECT   INCORRECT

Fig. 5-5. Triangle adjustment.

Connect the vertical input of the oscilloscope to the triangle output of the VCO and adjust trimmer R19 until the two sides of the waveform meet at the top, as shown in Fig. 5-5.

Connect a +5V bias supply to one of the control inputs of the VCO. Monitor this voltage with the VOM by connecting its positive lead to the +5V BIAS jack and the negative lead to ground; set the VOM to the 2.5V range.

Connect the vertical input of the oscilloscope to the TRIANGLE output of the oscillator and the horizontal input to the output of the signal generator. Set the oscilloscope for external horizontal input. At this point the equipment should be interconnected as shown in Fig. 5-6 (in the drawing, the power supply is shown as 2720-7; this number designates the PAIA modular supply.)

Set the output of the +5V bias supply to 0.625V as indicated on the VOM. Set the signal generator to 260 Hz (approximately middle C in the musical scale) and use the ZERO adjust of the VCO (R4) to produce the figure-8 waveform shown in Fig. 5-7. This Lissajous figure indicates that the output of the signal generator is exactly twice the frequency of the VCO. Do not be overly concerned with a slow rotation of the pattern.

Adjust the +5V bias supply until the oscilloscope displays the pattern shown, indicating that the output of the signal generator is one-half the output frequency of the VCO.

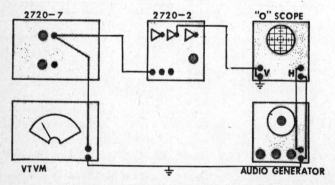

Fig. 5-6. Equipment interconnection.

Fig. 5-7. Bow-tie Lissajous figure.

Read the VOM. If the reading is less than 2.5V rotate RANGE trimmer (R7) about $^1/_{10}$ turn counterclockwise.

Reset the bias output to 0.625V and once again adjust the ZERO trimmer to produce the Lissajous figure.

Repeat steps 6 through 8 until the VOM reading is 2.5V. On each succeeding pass the adjustment of the RANGE trimmer should be less, corresponding to the decreasing error between the actual reading of the VOM and the ideal 2.5V.

Calibration Method 2. For this procedure, you'll need a tuned musical instrument (piano or organ would be best), amplifier, and voltohmmeter (VOM).

Connect the pulse output of the VCO to the high (line) level input of the amplifier. Turn PULSE DURATION control fully to the right. Connect the 0 to 5V bias supply to the left-hand control voltage input jack of the VCO and use the VOM to monitor this voltage. Set the VOM for 2.5V range.

Set the bias supply for 0.625V and press the C below middle C key on the reference instrument. Use the ZERO adjust of the VCO (R4) for zero-beat between the pitch of the VCO and the reference instrument.

Press the C above middle C key on the reference instrument and adjust the 5V bias supply so that the output of the VCO is zero-beat with this pitch.

Read the VOM. If the reading is less than 2.5V rotate the RANGE trimmer (R7) about $^1/_{10}$ turn clockwise. If the reading is greater than 2.5V rotate the trimmer about $^1/_{10}$ turn counterclockwise.

Reset the bias output to 0.625V and once again adjust the ZERO trimmer to zero-beat with C below middle C.

Repeat steps until VOM reading is 2.5V.

Set the bias control for approximately 1.0V and turn the PULSE DURATION control fully counterclockwise. Adjust trimmer R26 until the buzz of the pulse output can just barely be heard.

Transfer the output from the PULSE output jack to the TRIANGLE output jack and adjust R20 for the mellowest possible tone.

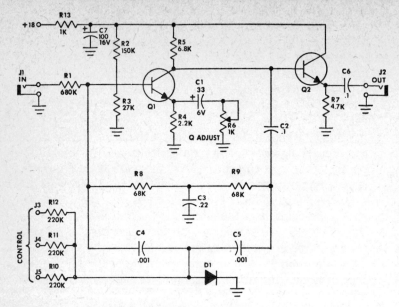

Fig. 5-8. Bandpass filter schematic.

FILTERS

The PAIA engineers looked at a lot of filters while they were designing their 2720 synthesizer modules and reported that some of the specs were "enough to make your head swim": center and cutoff frequency ranges running up to 20 octaves, filters that tracked a control voltage with errors of only 0.02%, phenomenal Q's, and lots more.

But when they started playing with these filters, they discovered an interesting thing: you pay a lot for specifications; in general, the added usefulness is not proportional to the added cost. The average user is after *sound* that he can produce with a synthesizer and is not so interested in being able to exactly calculate a mathematical analysis of sound.

Based on this, careful and considered compromises have been made in the filters. For instance, the range of the bandpass filter of Fig. 5-8 is limited. A professional user able to compare this device to the $300 filters of a large synthesizer could easily tell the difference. Similarly, the filters will not *exactly* track the keyboard voltage.

What the filters *will* do is provide you with an economical means of controlling the harmonic content of a synthesized sound and allow you to change the harmonic content using control voltages generated by control oscillators, function generators, or manual controllers.

Three pin jacks (J3, J4, and J5) allow the summation of up to three control voltage sources. As the algebraic sum of the inputs to these jacks increases, the center frequency of the filter is shifted up. The highest possible center frequency is achieved when the algebraic sum of the inputs is 5V but negative voltages and potentials greater than 5V will not harm the unit. As the algebraic sum of the inputs to the three comparable jacks of the low-pass filter (Fig. 5-9) increases, the rolloff rate of the filter increases. The highest rolloff rate—12 dB/octave—is reached when the control voltages sum to 5V.

Voltage-Controlled Bandpass Filter

The voltage-controlled bandpass filter provides a compact, inexpensive, and easily controlled means of varying the dynamic timbral properties of synthesized sounds. Features of this filter include summing control voltage inputs and variable Q control.

Design Analysis. Resistors R8 and R9 in combination with capacitors C3, C4, and C5, and the equivalent impedance of diode D1 form a parallel-tee notch filter in the feedback loop of the common-emitter gain stage (Q1). The combination of gain with a notch filter in the negative feedback path produces a bandpass filter.

As the voltages applied to the three input jacks increase, the total current flow through R10, R11, R12, and D1 increases. As the current flow through the diode increases, its equivalent impedance decreases; this causes the center frequency of the filter section's notch to increase. As the center frequency of the notch increases, the center frequency of the amplifier/filter combination also increases.

Potentiometer R6 varies the gain of the Q1 stage by varying the amount of signal bypassed through C1 at the Q1 emitter. An increase of the gain of this stage increases the amplitude of the signals that are passed through the amplifier, which has the effect of increasing the Q of the filter. Buffer Q2 isolates the filter from the loading effects of successive stages.

The time constants of the notch filter section have been carefully chosen to provide maximum center-frequency range and the flattest possible response over that range. In special cases, the range can be changed by proportionally altering the values of C3, C4, and C5.

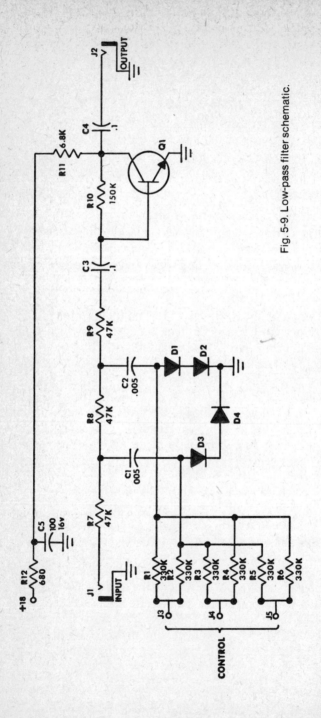

Fig. 5-9. Low-pass filter schematic.

Halving the values of these capacitors will double both the high and low ends of the filter range; and doubling the values will halve both the high and the low end. Under no circumstances should the values of R8 and R9 be changed.

Testing. The bandpass filter may be tested using only an audio signal source (preferably square wave) and an audio amplifier.

Connect a power supply to the power connections to supply +18V. Connect the pulse output of the VCO to the input of the filter and set the pulse width to minimum. Apply approximately 2.5V to one of the control inputs of the VCO so that the output frequency of the oscillator is about 600 Hz. Connect the output of the bandpass filter to the high-level input of an audio amplifier.

Connect a ±5V bias supply to one of the control inputs of the bandpass filter. Advance the filter's Q control fully clockwise and turn up the amplifier to a comfortable listening level.

Vary the ±5V bias supply between about 0 and +5V and observe that the changes in the control voltage produce a *wah-wah* sound. Observe that as the Q control is rotated in a counterclockwise direction the wah-wah effect is less pronounced.

The Bandpass Amplifier in Practical Operation. Voltage-controlled filters are an excellent example of apparatus in which the cost and precision and the temptation to play "specsmanship" are both high.

The circuit is designed as a low-cost module and some design compromises have been made. For instance, the summation of the control voltages is not exact. Because of the use of a passive summation network there is a maximum possible error of about 5%.

As with any filter, the circuit is primarily intended for use in modifying the harmonic content of harmonic-rich waveforms such as square, pulse, ramp, and noise. In these applications, the control voltage can come from any of the standard control voltage sources such as the control oscillator or function generator for swept filter effects. The control voltage can also be used to set the parameters of the filter, providing a higher bandpass center frequency as higher notes are played.

One of the most interesting applications is voicing the output of the noise source. Typical of the sounds produced with this combination is the whistle of the wind. Connect the output of the noise source into the input of the bandpass filter and the output of the filter to the input of the amplifier being used. Use a bias supply for the control voltage to the filter's control inputs. When the filter is set to a high Q the wind can be heard to whistle as the bias supply varies. For additional realism, the second bias supply can be used to control the VCA which is put between the filter output and amplifier input.

Noise can be substituted for a more standard pitch signal source using the noise source/filter combination described above. In this case the control voltage for the filter comes from the controller and the output of the filter goes into other processing modules for envelope shaping, etc. The pitch of the noise will not exactly correspond to the pitch produced by the controller/VCO combination, but by turning the PITCH knob of the controller fully counterclockwise and biasing the filter slightly, you can come close.

Voltage-Controlled Low-Pass Filter

The voltage-controlled low-pass filter provides an automatically controllable means of varying the higher frequency content of a waveform. This module finds its greatest use as a voltage-variable tone control and as an element for converting a triangle wave to a sine wave.

Design Analysis. The circuit shown represents one of the least sophisticated filter designs imaginable. Resistors R7, R8, and R9 in combination with capacitors C1 and C2 form a standard pi-section low-pass filter. The equivalent impedances of diodes D1 through D4 in the legs of the network set the maximum rejection of the filter as well as determining the frequency at which the filter begins to roll off.

As increasing voltages are applied to the control input jacks (J3 through J5) they cause a greater current flow through resistors R1—R6 and consequently through diodes D1—D4. As the current flow through the diodes increases, their equivalent impedance decreases, causing the rejection ratio to increase and the cutoff frequency to roll back.

The single common-emitter gain stage (Q1) serves to isolate the filter section from the loading effects of most output terminations and provides slight gain to overcome the losses of the filter section.

In special cases the cutoff frequency of the filter can be adjusted by changing the values of capacitors C1 and C2. Doubling the values of these capacitors will approximately halve the cutoff frequency; halving their values will approximately double the cutoff frequency.

Testing. The circuit may be tested using only an audio signal source and an audio amplifier.

Supply +18V power to the module. Jumper the signal source to the input of the module and the output of the module to the line level input of the amplifier. Adjust the volume of the amplifier for a comfortable listening level.

Using a ±5V bias supply, apply a 0−5V control voltage to jacks J3, J4, and J5 in turn. Observe that as the control voltage is increased, the sound from the amplifier becomes less raspy and more bassy.

Using the Low-Pass Filter. The purpose of any low-pass filter is to eliminate or attenuate frequencies above some cutoff frequency. In most voltage control filters the control voltage is used to either vary this cutoff frequency or vary the amount by which frequencies above the cutoff are attenuated.

With zero control voltage applied to the filter there is virtually no insertion loss through the filter at any operating frequency. As the sum of three control voltages is increased, the cutoff frequency begins to roll back and the rejection ratio above the cutoff frequency begins to increase. At the maximum control voltage of 5V, frequencies above 500 Hz are rejected by 12 dB for every octave increase in frequency.

This design for a filter is somewhat unusual in its simplicity but the design constraints originally imposed on this module were primarily economic. The average user will be more interested in the sound he can produce than in the technical specifications of the modules themselves; the circuit shown is quite adequate for the cost.

Control voltages for the filter can originate from any of the standard control voltage sources such as a control oscillator for swept frequency effects. Or the voltage from the controller can be applied to the filter to increase the rolloff and lower the cutoff frequency as higher notes are played. The control voltage can originate in the function generator, provided the attack times are not too short. The low-pass filter has a tendency to pop if the control voltage changes too rapidly.

Filter parameters can also be biased using ±5V supplies. These same bias supplies can be used to set the filter to a constant cutoff frequency.

FUNCTION GENERATOR

A common feature of many function generators is the attack-release-sustain-decay output used in synthesizing certain percussion sounds. A single module such as that shown

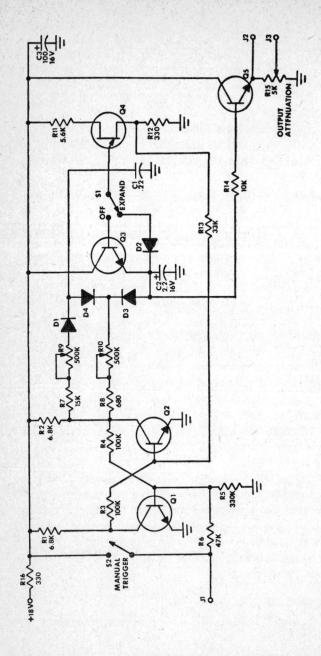

Fig. 6-10. Function generator schematic.

in Fig. 5-10 does not offer this function—not because it is not desirable but because the cost of adding it would almost double the price of the module while only adding one feature.

If there were no way to produce the attack-release-sustain-decay waveform other than using a special module, PAIA's engineers would have designed the module regardless of the cost; but as it happens this function can be generated using two identical circuits (Fig. 5-10). The cost of two modules is only slightly greater than what the cost of the more elaborate single module would have been and the added versatility is great.

Figure 5-11 shows how this is accomplished. The controller (designated 2720-6) has two trigger outputs: a short-duration pulse that is generated whenever any key is pressed and a voltage step that is turned on when a key is pressed and off when the key is released. The pulse can be used to trigger one of the function generators (designated 2720-4 in the drawing) that is responsible for the attack and release portion of the wave. The second 2720-4 is triggered from the step output and produces the sustain and decay part of the wave as well as contributing to the attack. In the commercial synthesizer from which these circuits were borrowed, the outputs of the two function generators are run to the control inputs of a single module (VCA typically), where they are summed together as

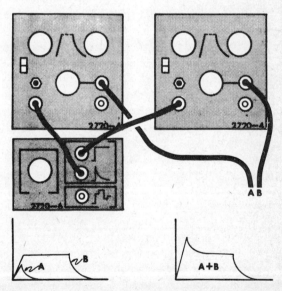

Fig. 5-11. Making an attack-release-sustain-decay waveform.

shown in the drawings. Note particularly that the setting of the variable output attenuator of the second module determines the sustain level and that the peak level of the attack is the sum of the output of the two function generators. For optimum performance this sum should not exceed 5V.

Not only do you have a greater range of control over the function when two modules are used but you have the capability of using them separately. For instance, one to generate dynamics while the other makes time-varying timbral changes.

The MANUAL TRIGGER pushbutton is provided for testing the function generator and to provide a means of triggering the module without using a controller. When MANUAL TRIGGER is pressed, the output of the generator will rise at a rate set by the ATTACK control and will remain at that level until the button is released. The MANUAL TRIGGER button should not be used when another trigger source is plugged into the TRIGGER jack; no damage would result but the output under this condition would not meet full specifications.

Design Analysis

The function generator provides the synthesizer with a triggerable source of time-varying voltage useful in automatically controlling filters, oscillators, and amplifiers. Controls allow independent adjustment of the function's attack time, decay time, and overall amplitude. Both electrical and manual triggers are provided for.

In Fig. 5-10, Q1 and Q2 form a bistable multivibrator that, in its normal condition, has Q2 held on. In response to an input trigger applied to the base of Q1, Q2 switches off and its collector voltage rises to the supply voltage. C1 can now charge from the current through R7, R9, and D1 at a rate determined by the setting of ATTACK control R9. With S1 in the normal position, the voltage across C1 is applied to the base of emitter follower Q3, which in turn supplies a charging current to C2. Since the current required to charge C2 is supplied by Q3, the voltage across this capacitor is dependent only on the time constant associated with C1.

Even though the value of C2 is 50 times that of C1, it can charge at essentially the time constant of C1. At some period of time the voltage across C1 reaches the threshold of Q4 and the unijunction transistor fires, causing C1 to discharge and a pulse to appear across R12. The pulse, applied to the base of Q2 through R13, resets the bistable and causes collector voltage of

Q2 to go to ground. C2 does not discharge through Q4 because it is isolated by Q3; but with the collector of Q2 at ground, C2 can discharge through R8, R10, and D3 at a rate determined by the setting of DECAY control R10. Diodes D1 and D3 assure that the charging current is supplied only through R9 and the discharging current only through R10. The voltage across capacitor C2, isolated by buffer Q5, becomes the envelope output.

When S1 is switched to EXPAND it isolates emitter follower Q3 and connects C2 in parallel with C1, thereby making the charging time constant about 50 times greater. With S1 in this position, D2 reverse-biases as C1 discharges through Q4 so that C2 still only discharges through the DECAY control R10.

If a step, rather than a pulse, is used as a trigger, the sequences up to the discharging of C1 are the same, but now the bistable will not stay in its reset mode and C2 cannot discharge. Q4 now functions as a standard unijunction relaxation oscillator that keeps trying to reset the bistable until the trigger is removed. In the expanded position of S1, D2 isolates C1 from the fully charged C2 so that even though the first charging cycle takes place at a rate determined by the parallel combination of C1 and C2, subsequent cycles occur at the time constant of C1 alone.

Testing

The function generator can be tested either with an oscilloscope or a VOM. Begin by hooking an 18V power supply to the supply connections on the rear edge of the circuit board. If an oscilloscope is available, it is the preferred testing method. Connect the vertical input to the variable output of the function generator. With the variable output attenuator rotated fully clockwise, check to make sure the output rises to +5V when the manual TRIGGER button is pressed and stays at that level as long as the button is held down. If the time base of the scope is calibrated, check to make sure that the rise and fall times compare with the following table (allow ±20% for component tolerances):

ATTACK	EXPAND	DECAY	RISE	FALL
CCW	off	CCW	2 msec	5 msec
CW	off	CW	40 msec	1 sec
CCW	expand	CCW	30 msec	5 msec
CW	expand	CW	1 sec	1 sec

Test the output attenuator by rotating it CCW and observing that the amplitude of the output waveform decreases to zero.

Connect the vertical input of the scope to the 5V peak-to-peak function generator output and observe that the output is present at this jack and that it has a peak value of +5V.

If a scope is not available, the module may be tested with a VOM by connecting the positive lead to the variable output and measuring the output with the manual TRIGGER button depressed. With ATTACK and DECAY controls both rotated fully CW, observe that the output takes approximately 1 sec to rise to +5V and that the output remains at that level as long as the button is held down. Release the button and observe that the voltage takes about 1 sec to fall to about the 0.5V level (the decay is on an exponential curve, so never reaches zero.) With the manual TRIGGER button held down observe that the variable output is varied as the attenuator is rotated in a clockwise direction. Measure the voltage at the 5V peak-to-peak output and observe that it is 5V.

The Function Generator in Practical Operation

The function generator is one of the most useful single building blocks in a synthesizer. It is also the module most likely to be duplicated as the system is expanded. The circuit is less elaborate than many function generators in that there is no sustain level control. The sustain level control was omitted for simplicity. Execution of the circuitry required for such a control would have increased the potential cost by about 60% and the sustain is only used a small portion of the time.

There are a large number of sound parameters that enable a person to distinguish one musical instrument from another, but chief among these are attack and decay—how fast the sound builds up and dies away.

Perfect examples of these characteristics can be illustrated by flutes and drums. Everyone knows that a flute doesn't sound anything like a drum, but the fact is that the basic waveshape of both instruments is very close to a sine wave. A flute has a relatively long attack by the standards of most instruments because it takes a certain amount of time for the vibrations of the air mass in the body of the flute to build up. A drum, on the other hand, immediately produces its maximum amplitude as soon as the head is struck. A flute sustains for as long as the musician can keep his wind, the drum sound begins to decay immediately. These are the only things which give the drum its hard sound as opposed to the soft sound of the flute.

The function generator is the module which supplies the control voltage necessary to produce these dynamic volume changes as well as the dynamic timbral changes (changes in harmonic content of the waveform) that set apart piano, guitar, and other percussive stringed instruments.

Routing the output of the function generator into the control inputs of the VCA permits the creation of a wide variety of volume dynamics, while the combination of function generator and VCF produces varying timbral changes.

It is possible to trigger the function generator from the keyboard and control oscillator. It is also possible to trigger a function generator from the output of another function generator. In this arrangement, the output of the second function generator will be at 0V for some time after the first generator is triggered. When the output of the first generator reaches the 3V level required to trigger the second generator, it will produce its own attack and decay parameters. The length of time before the second generator is triggered is adjustable using the attack and variable output controls of the first generator.

There are some instruments whose dynamics cause the sound to rapidly rise to a peak and then, over some ordinarily short period of time, decay to a sustain level which is maintained as long as the note is held. This effect is achieved with two function generators. In the case of the keyboard, one of the function generators is triggered from the keyboard pulse output and the second from the step output. The initial attack and decay characteristics are set by the function generator being triggered from the pulse and sustain, and final decay characteristics are set by the generator being triggered by the step. The outputs of each of these modules is routed to two of the control inputs of the particular processing modules being used—the VCA for example. The variable output of the second function generator is used to set the sustain level and the variable output of the second generator is used to make up the difference between the sustain level and the 5V maximum control input of the VCA.

CONTROL OSCILLATOR/NOISE SOURCE

Control oscillator/noise source may seem like a strange combination, but there is good reasoning behind it. Most importantly, neither of these two circuits is likely to be repeated within any one system; one of each is necessary but usually sufficient.

Secondly, the required circuitry and front panel controls of the two lend themselves to the combination. Both require only single-module circuit boards, but the oscillator needs a double module front panel to properly arrange the controls. The single output jack of the noise source can be just about anywhere. The circuitry used in PAIA's 2720 synthesizer is shown in Fig. 5-12.

The noise source has been mentioned as being necessary for the synthesis of snare drums, cymbals, wind, and surf; but it is instructive to understand exactly what noise is.

If you turn on an FM radio and set it between two stations you will hear noise of the type produced by depicted module (2720-5). This familiar hissing sound is the result of summing together all audio frequencies, each of which has its own random amplitude variations.

Color references are ordinarily used as a qualitative measure of the frequency content of the noise. If *all* frequencies are distributed within the signal (as in the FM example), then the noise is called *white* (drawing a parallel between it and white light, which consists of all colors). If only the lower frequencies are included in the signal the noise is referred to as pink. Many synthesizers provide color control directly on the noise source front panel, but this is to a certain extent redundant since the voltage-controlled filters can serve the same purpose.

The control oscillator can be used as a trigger source for the function generator to produce a combined element capable of producing a wide range of repeating waveforms.

Design Analysis

The 2720-5 control oscillator/noise source is a dual-function module providing a source of slowly varying sinusoidal control voltage for tremolo, vibrato, filter sweeping, etc. plus a white noise source useful in a variety of special effects including wind and surf sounds.

Control Oscillator. The control oscillator circuit is a common phase-shift type with transistor Q1 providing gain and 180° phase shift while the remaining 180° of required phase shift is provided by the pi network composed of C1—C9 and R4, R5, and R17—R19. Buffer Q2 isolates the load from the oscillator stage.

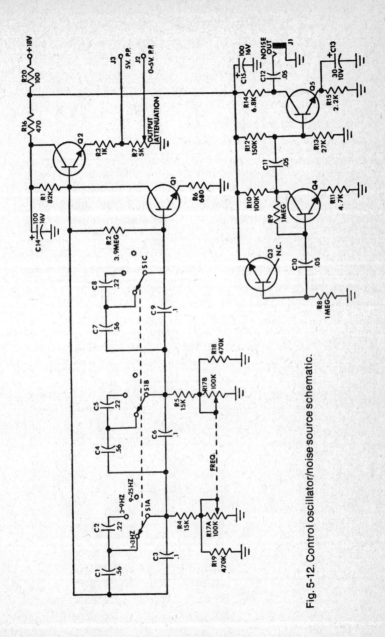

Fig. 5-12. Control oscillator/noise source schematic.

167

The only thing unusual about the design is the switching of capacitors C1—C9. Referring to the schematic diagram, you can see that in the 1—3 Hz position of S1, C1 is in parallel with C3, C4 with C6, and C7 with C9. In this position the total capacitance in each branch of the pi network is 0.66 μF.

In the 3—9 Hz position the series combination of C1 and C2 is in parallel with C3, C4 and C5 in parallel with C6, and C7 and C8 in parallel with C9. This arrangement gives a total capacitance of approximately 0.2 μF. In the 9—25 Hz position, C3, C6, and C9 are the only capacitors in the circuit for a total capacitance in each branch of 0.1 μF.

Noise Source. As can be seen from the schematic diagram, the noise source is a very simple circuit. Transistor Q3 is a silicon type that has a low emitter-to-base breakdown voltage rating. The 18V supply is more than enough to cause this base—emitter junction to operate in an avalanche condition.

Resistor R8 in the base circuit of Q3 limits the current flow through the junction and also serves as a load resistor for the shot noise that results from the avalanche process. The random AC voltage fluctuations produced by the avalanche are coupled into a single common-emitter amplifier stage (Q4) through capacitor C11. This first stage not only boosts the signal slightly but serves as an impedance-matching element between the noise source and main amplifier Q5. The amplified noise is coupled by C12 to the OUTPUT jack.

Oscillator Testing

Apply 18V power. The control oscillator is most easily tested using an oscilloscope, but a voltohmmeter can be used. If an oscilloscope is available connect its vertical input to the fixed 5V p-p output of the oscillator and observe that the output is approximately 5V. If the oscilloscope has a calibrated horizontal time scale, check to make sure that the periods of oscillation agree with the table below at the control settings indicated.

S1	R17	PERIOD
		1 sec
		330 msec
1—3	CCW (min)	350 msec
1—3	CW (max)	350 msec
3—9	Min	120 msec
3—9	Max	120 msec
9—25	Min	125 msec
9—25	Max	45 msec

Due to component tolerances, exact agreement is unlikely but observed periods should be within 20% of the above values. With this check completed connect the oscilloscope vertical input to the variable output (J2) and observe that attenuator R7 varies the output from 0V to 5V peak-to-peak. When observing the oscillator waveform on an oscilloscope, you may note a slight flattening on the bottom of the sine wave. This flattening is normal and will not significantly affect the operation of the unit.

Operation of the oscillator can be roughly checked as follows: Set the VOM to 10V range and connect the meter between the ground and fixed output with the positive lead to J3. Set *frequency range* switch S1 to the 1−3 Hz range and rotate FREQ control R17 fully counterclockwise. Most meters will not accurately follow a 1 Hz signal but you should be able to see the pointer swinging up and down, and the extremes of the swing should center about the 2.5V mark on the meter. Advance the FREQ control and note that the rate of oscillation increases. As switch S1 and the FREQ control are advanced, the meter pointer should move less and less until at some point it stops (at about 2.5V). Now change the positive meter lead to variable output J2 and observe that the attenuator varies the output level from 0V to about 2.5V.

Noise Source Testing

The noise source is easily tested using either an audio amplifier or an oscilloscope. If an oscilloscope is available, connect NOISE OUT jack J1 to the vertical input of the scope and observe that the peak-to-peak amplitude of the characteristically fuzzy noise signal is approximately 0.5V. The noise effect is best observed with a sweep rate of about 2 msec/cm (repetition rate of about 50 per second on scopes without a calibrated time base). If an amplifier is handy, the output of the noise source can be connected directly to the high-level input of the amplifier. Test for an even coloration of the noise by alternately advancing and retarding the bass and treble tone controls of the amplifier. During this test the character of the noise will change noticeably (this will also depend on the characteristics of the amplifier's tone control).

POWER SUPPLY

The 2720-7 power supply (Fig. 5-13) does more than simply supply power to the rest of the modules. Occasions arise where the output of standard control voltage sources do not lend

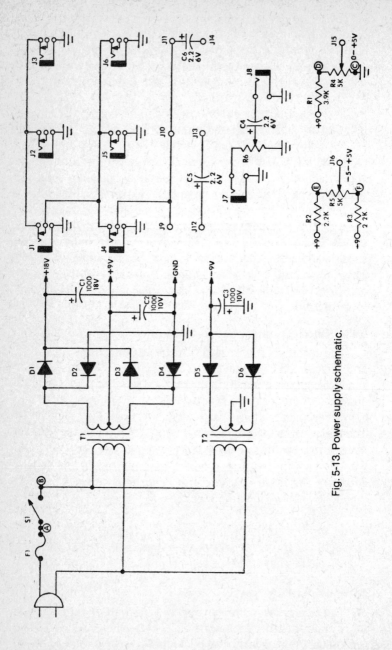

Fig. 5-13. Power supply schematic.

themselves to the effect desired. For instance, there will be many times that you want to shift a filter over only part of its range. The high-control-voltage end of the range can be decreased simply by using an attenuator, but if you want to bring up the low end you need to bias the filter by summing in a *constant* control voltage. For cases such as this the power supply module has two variable-voltage bias supplies. These bias supplies also provide a means of manually controlling slowly varying voltage-controlled parameters.

There are times when the output of a control voltage source will need to be routed to more than one processing module—as when the control voltage is not only setting the pitch of the VCO but the parameters of one of the filters. The power supply circuit shown provides for this with a multiple access patch panel consisting of 12 jacks (the PAIA unit has six pin jacks and six miniature phone jacks). One of the features of the patch panel is a switching system that conditionally connects together all of the phone jacks and the first row of pin jacks. Inserting a phone plug in the first jack of either row of phone jacks isolates that row from the row directly below it. The phone jacks and pin jacks can be used as isolated rows or in a number of combinations. The placement of two capacitors in this panel allows their use as isolating elements when patching external musical instruments into the console.

An isolated front-panel attenuator can be used as a master volume control, mixing level adjustment, or as an attenuator for external instruments.

The 0−5V and −5 to +5V bias supplies should be controlled by panel knobs. Clockwise rotation of the control knob increases the voltage available at the associated pin jack.

Design Analysis

The actual power supply consists of two separate full-wave rectifiers. One section (T1, D1−D4, C1, and C2) provides the 18V and 9V supplies, while the other (T2, D5, D6, and C3) supplies the −9V. Regulation is not included because only the VCO requires a regulated supply and regulation is included with that circuit.

Testing

There is really not much to test on the power supply. Once it is plugged in, use a VOM to check all of the available voltages. Double-check the wiring of the switching plugs to insure that they are wired as shown in the schematic.

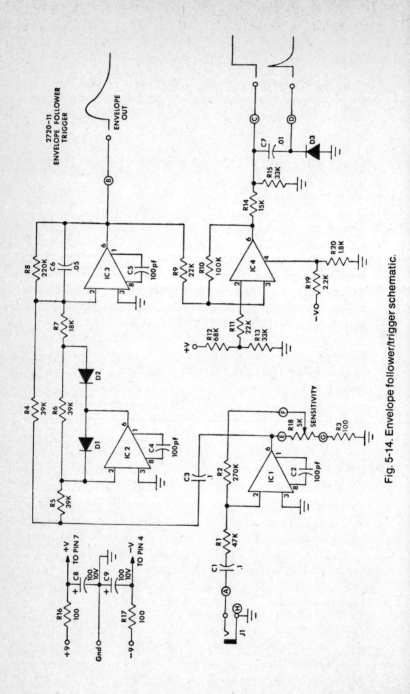

Fig. 5-14. Envelope follower/trigger schematic.

Using the Power Supply

The power supply does a little more than supply power to the rest of a system. It provides two sources of variable voltage, an audio and control voltage patch panel, and an audio attenuator.

ENVELOPE FOLLOWER/TRIGGER

The biggest problem associated with using the 2720 series modules to process the outputs of conventional musical instruments is the loss of the triggering functions that are ordinarily provided by the 2720 keyboard. Without these triggering functions, much of the automation that makes a synthesizer a practical reality is lost.

The envelope follower trigger overcomes this problem by converting the amplitude contour of any instrument into a high-level control voltage and provides step and pulse trigger outputs derived from the instrument's output.

Design Analysis

For ease of analysis the circuit (Fig. 5-14) can be divided into three essentially independent sections; an input amplifier, a full-wave rectifier, and a Schmitt trigger.

Signals applied to input jack J1 are amplified by operational amplifier IC1. Gain of this stage is variable from 15 dB to 34 dB, depending on how much of the output signal is tapped off by potentiometer R18 and applied to the feedback resistor R2. The output of this amplifier drives the full-wave rectifier.

Input signals to the rectifier are applied simultaneously to the inverting inputs of both IC2 (by way of R5) and IC3 (by R4). Assuming that the input is a sine wave, negative half-cycles applied to the inverting input of IC2 cause the output of this amplifier to try to drive positive. As soon as the output reaches a voltage above ground that is equal to the forward voltage drop of D1, that diode begins to conduct and clamps the output at that voltage. At the same time diode D2 reverse-biases and isolates the output of IC2 from the rest of the circuit so that there is no input to IC3 through R7. The input through R4 causes the output of IC3 to go positive.

For positive half-cycles of the input, the output of IC2 goes negative, which reverse-biases D1 (thereby eliminating it from the circuit) and forward-biases D2. In this condition there are two inputs to IC3: a positive input through R4 and an equal-amplitude (because of the ratio of IC-2). These two inputs

173

are supplied by the output of IC2. These two inputs are summed together; if R7 and R4—the summing resistors—were equal values, the inputs would cancel completely. But since the value of R7 is approximately half that of R4, the net result is a positive voltage at the output of IC3. The ratio of R8 to R4 and R7 provides additional gain in the rectifier while C6 produces a low-pass response that averages the output. The rectifier output is available as a control voltage proportional to the amplitude of the low-level input envelope and is also applied to the Schmitt trigger built around IC4.

The design of the trigger circuit is in most respects a common type with the input signal applied through R9 to the noninverting input of the opamp, where it is compared with the reference voltage produced at the junction of voltage divider R12, R13. Positive feedback for hysteresis is supplied by R10. Trigger points are set at approximately 3V for the high threshold and 2V for the low threshold.

The step output should be close to ground when the trigger is off, but a normal Schmitt configuration would produce an output near the negative supply voltage. There are a number of ways that a diode could be used to clamp the output at ground but all of them draw unnecessarily large amounts of current. Returning the negative supply pin of IC4 to ground won't work, since the maximum output swing of an opamp is limited to something less than the supply voltages (the *off* state of the trigger would be several volts positive). For these reasons the negative supply of IC4 is derived from the voltage divider consisting of R19 and R20 and is set to be below ground by a voltage corresponding to the difference between the maximum output swing and supply.

The output step of the Schmitt trigger is attenuated by a voltage divider (R14, R15). The pulse trigger is formed from the voltage step by the differentiating action of C7, and diode D3 is provided to clamp negative pulses to ground.

Testing

There are no internal adjustments to make. The only test equipment required will be a VOM and an amplitude-variable audio signal generator.

Connect the unit to a power supply. With no signal applied to the input of the module, use the VOM to make sure that there is no voltage present at either the *envelope* or *pulse trigger* outputs. Similarly, check for voltage at the *step trigger* output.

It will be normal to find a very small negative or positive voltage at the step output, but it should be less than 1V.

Next, apply the amplitude-variable signal source to the input. Set the signal generator for approximately 440 Hz and set the envelope follower SENSITIVITY control fully counterclockwise. With the VOM connected to the envelope output pin jack observe that as the amplitude of the signal source is varied between 0 and 0.5V p-p, the voltage at the output varies between 0 and 5V. Connect the VOM to the *step trigger* output and slowly increase the amplitude of the input signal until the instant a voltage appears at this output. The voltage at the step output should be 5V and the voltage at the envelope output should be 3V.

Once again, connect the VOM to the *step output* jack and slowly reduce the amplitude of the input signal until the instant the step output returns to 0V. Read the envelope output voltage and observe that it is 2V ($\pm 10\%$).

With the VOM still connected to the envelope output and the SENSITIVITY control fully counterclockwise, set the amplitude of the signal source for a reading of 0.25V on the meter. Observe that by rotating the SENSITIVITY control clockwise the envelope output voltage can be raised to 7V or greater.

Using the Envelope Follower/Trigger

The inputs to the 2720 series processing modules (amplifiers, filters, etc.) must always be AC coupled to whatever signal source is being used. When the various modules are simply feeding each other, this requirement is taken care of by the capacitively coupled outputs of the modules themselves. But when a conventional instrument is being used as a feed for the system the coupling capacitor must be externally supplied. Isolating capacitors are provided as part of the patch panel associated with the power supply. The input to the envelope follower is isolated by its own internal coupling capacitor.

SINE CONVERTER/PULSE WIDTH MODULATOR

The sine converter/pulse width modulator accepts a triangular wave input with a peak-to-peak amplitude of 400 to 900 mV and produces a sinusoidal waveform and a pulse with voltage-controllable duty factor.

A sine wave is the only "pure" tone and, as such, is appropriate for a number of musical applications either in simulation of natural instrument voices or as a completely electronic sound.

The effect of changing the width of a pulse is to vary both its harmonic structure and the phase relationships of those harmonics. As with other processing modules, voltage control allows automatic time-varying timbral changes that would be extremely difficult to produce if nothing but manual control were available.

Design Analysis

The circuitry is designed around an IC quad current differencing amplifier package. The schematic is shown in Fig. 5-15. When a triangular waveform is applied to the module, it is buffered and amplified by the first gain blocks in the package before being applied to the pulse width modulator and the sine converter. The trimmer in the input of this first stage (R32) allows the gain of the stage to be varied to compensate for level differences of the signal source.

The pulse width modulator is essentially a summing comparator. The current produced by the voltage appearing

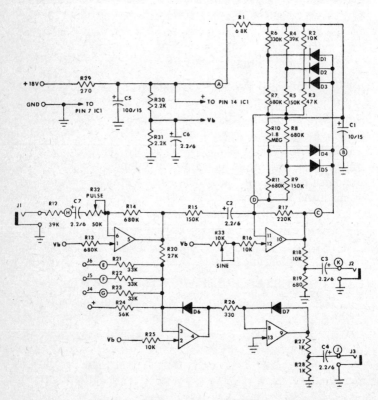

Fig. 5-15. Sine converter/pulse width modulator schematic.

across R20 (the triangular output of the first amplifier) is added to the sum of the currents produced by the control voltages that appear across R21, R22, and R23. This total current flow into the inverting input of the second amplifier is compared to the reference current flowing into the noninverting input through R25.

As long as the reference current into the input is greater than the total current flowing into the inverting input, the output of the amplifier stays high. Resistor values are selected so that for a small part of each cycle of the triangle, the current into the inverting input exceeds the reference current (causing the output to switch low). This produces a very narrow output pulse for zero control voltage. As the control voltages begin to rise from ground, the total current into the inverting input of the amplifier increases, causing progressively lower points on the triangle to switch the comparator. Since points further down the sides of the triangle are further apart, the net result is a pulse whose width increases in proportion to increases in control voltage.

As the comparator switches on and off, it switches the third amplifier in the package, which inverts the pulse and serves to square up the rise and fall times. Diodes D6 and D7 clamp the outputs at about 1V, thereby restricting the maximum rise and consequently the effect of amplifier slew rate on the final pulse. These diodes also provide bias current to the inverting inputs of the amplifiers at times that they would otherwise be reverse-biased.

The sine shaper is a classic nonlinear feedback type with a diode-break-point feedback loop. Here we are approximating a sine wave with a series of straight-line segments, as shown in Fig. 5-16. Assume that we begin watching the sine converter at a point in time when the input triangle is ramping down from the midpoint of the waveform. Amplifier 4 is arranged in an inverting configuration so as the input is heading down, the

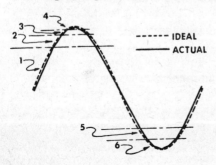

Fig. 5-16. Sine conversion.

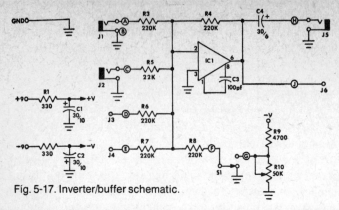

Fig. 5-17. Inverter/buffer schematic.

output is heading up. At the midpoint of the waveform all of the diodes in the sine converter (D1—D6) are reverse-biased so that the only element in the feedback loop is R17; this resistor alone determines the gain of the stage and, consequently, the rate at which the output voltage of the amplifier increases. This corresponds to line segment 1 in the figure.

Eventually the output voltage reaches the point at which it is greater than the voltage at the junction of the voltage divider consisting of R6 and R7. At this point, diode D1 forward-biases and parallels R7 with R17. This results in lower gain and a new line segment with a slower rate of increase than the previous segment. (This is segment 2.)

As the output voltage increases further it eventually reaches the point at which D2 is forward-biased, paralleling R5 with R7 and R17 (resulting in line segment 3). The process continues through line segment 4 and then proceeds in the other direction, progressively taking the parallel resistors out of the system. The result is a reasonably good sine wave.

INVERTER/BUFFER

The inverter/buffer (Fig. 5-17) seems, at first glance, to be one of the simplest and least useful of the processing modules. Simple it is...its only effect is to perform a 180° phase inversion on any signal applied to its inputs. Least useful it's not...in addition to the obvious control voltage inversion applications, the module can be used for filter convolution (changing high-pass to low-pass and bandpass to bandstop) and Q multiplication. A 20 dB input port allows the module to be used as a preamplifier when using the other modules as processing elements for conventional instruments with low-level outputs. And tandem control-voltage inputs provide for a low-offset-error inverting summer.

6 | Electronic Piano

No effort has been made to go into complete detail on the construction of an electronic piano. It is one of the possible inputs to a music synthesizer that would allow for some very special effects. It also illustrates very graphically how a waveform can be shaped using capacitors, resistors, and diodes. The circuit is shown in Fig. 6-1.

For a 61-note keyboard, 12 of these oscillator–divider circuits with one other single frequency are required. A total of 5 outputs are provided from each oscillator, making up a total of 60 notes.

The small printed-circuit keyboard in Fig. 6-2 can be used for any project in this book. Multiple boards of this design would serve as the keyboard for even the most complex synthesizer. Full-size keyboards are available from Pratt, Read & Co., Ivoryton, Connecticut 06442.

The voltage input to the circuit is supplied from V+ and should be +15–18V with respect to ground. The IC supply regulator supplies the flip-flops after being reduced and regulated by a zener diode. The oscillators are tuned to F$^{\#}$ (740 Hz) through F (1397 Hz). The resulting output is used directly for the top octave and successively divided to produce the lower octaves for each note. The key inputs are supplied from a keyboard by applying +15–18V to the inputs labeled KEY.

A photograph of various waveforms is shown in the following figures. In Fig. 6-3, the waveform at point X (Fig. 6-1) is shown from the time the key is pressed until it is released. Figure 6-3B and 6-3C show the waveform at point Y with and without *sustain* (a variable voltage from 0 to 18V applied to the input labeled SUSTAIN). Photo D shows the resulting signal on the collector of the output transistor Q3.

Photo E shows the sustained output (after Q8) for 110 Hz, and photo F shows the corresponding output for 55 Hz; finally, in photo G, a 55 Hz output is shown without sustain. The result is a very accurate approximation of piano sounds. The

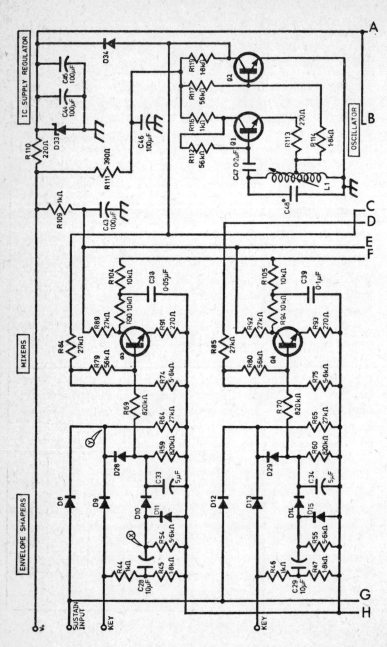

Fig. 6-1. Electronic piano circuit.

180

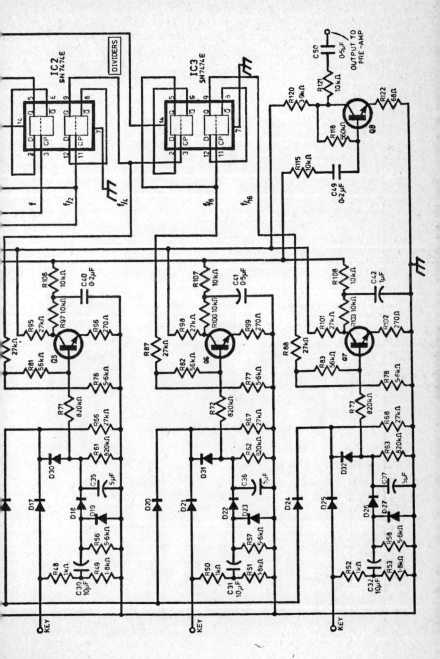

181

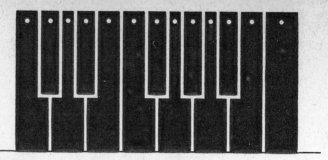

Fig. 6-2. Printed circuit keyboard.

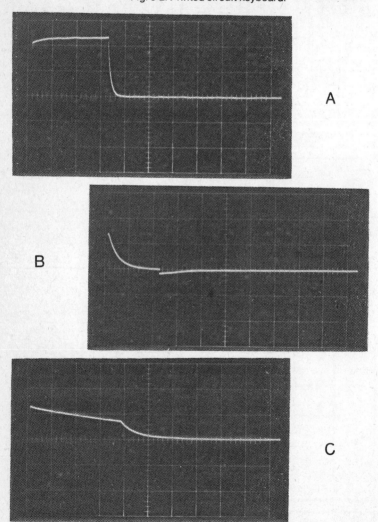

Fig. 6-3. Electronic piano output waveforms.

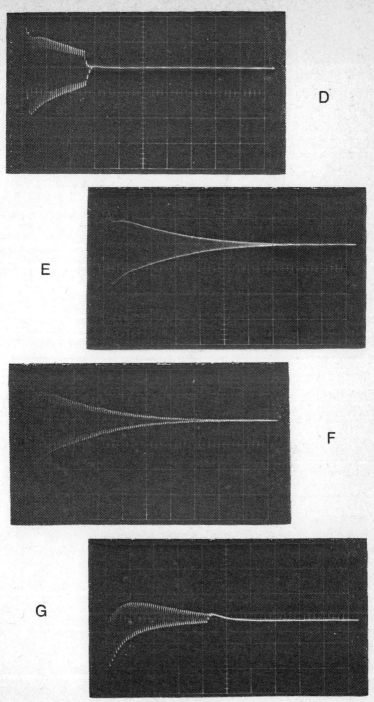

Fig. 6-3. Cont'd.

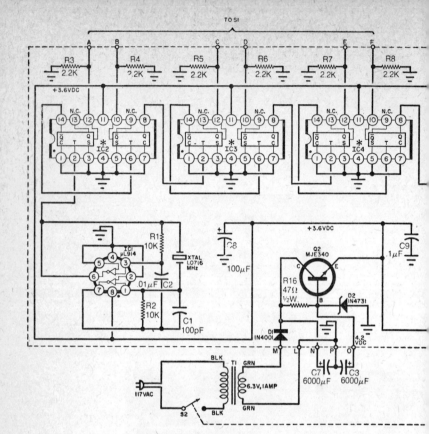

Fig. 6-4. Frequency divider.

oscillator could be a very stable multivibrator rather than the pot core oscillator shown.

PRECISION PITCH REFERENCE

In piano tuning, organ tuning or in the production of any kind of music, it is nice to have a source of at least one octave of the equally tempered scale that is known to be extremely accurate. For this reason a very accurate pitch reference is shown in the following figures.

A crystal oscillator operating at a frequency of 1.0716 MHz is used as a source. The notes required from C4 to B4 are shown in Table 6-1. The divisor required (division ratio) to produce the derived frequency from the 1.0716 MHz source is shown in the next column; the derived frequency is shown next; and finally, the standard frequency.

The resulting divider requires 12 stages to achieve successive binary divisions totaling 4096. In the next line, the

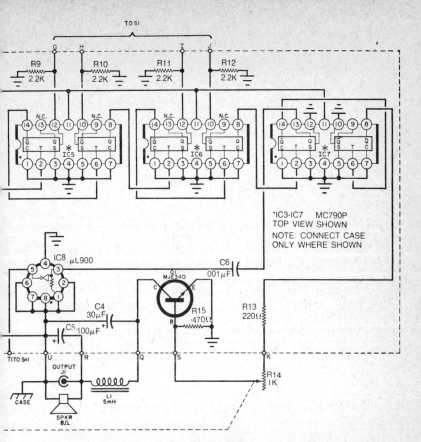

TO S1

*IC3-IC7   MC790P
TOP VIEW SHOWN
NOTE: CONNECT CASE
ONLY WHERE SHOWN

division ratio is 3866. This is 230 less than 4096 and requires that divisions by 2, 4, 32, 64, and 128 should be disabled or not done.

The divider in Fig. 6-4 attached to the switch in Fig. 6-5 accomplishes this division by doing exactly what the chart indicates. The divider, with the switch set at C4$^\sharp$ will actually divide by $1 + 8 + 16 + 256 + 1024 + 2048 = 3865$. This is 1 short of 3866, which is actually the case with each of the division ratios actually used.

With a crystal-controlled oscillator, a programmable divider, and some shaping circuits, a fairly good pitch reference can be obtained. Figure 6-6 is a full-size circuit card layout that will allow a circuit board to be made for this project. The circuit is shown in Fig. 6-4 and the switching arrangement in Fig. 6-5.

Table 6-1 will supply some interesting information in coping with the possibility of using the same type of circuitry for other purposes in a synthesizer.

Table 6-1. Pitch and Frequency Data.

PITCH	DIVISION RATIO	DERIVED FREQUENCY	STANDARD FREQUENCY	
C4	4096	261.6	261.6	0
C4#	3866	277.2	277.2	230
				2,4,32,64,128
D4	3650	293.6	293.7	446
				2,4,8,16,32,128,256
D4	3444	311.2	311.2	652
				4,8,128,512
E4	3250	329.7	329.6	846
				2,4,8,64,256,512
F4	3068	349.3	349.2	1028
				4,1024
F4	2896	370.0	370.0	1200
				16,32,128,1024
G4	2734	392.0	392.0	1362
				2,16,64,256,1024
G4	2580	415.4	415.3	1516
				4,8,32,64,128,256,1024
A4	2436	439.9	440.0	1660
				4,8,16,32,64,512,1024
A4	2298	466.3	466.2	1798
				2,4,256,512,1024
B4	2170	493.8	493.9	1926
				2,4,128,256,512,1024

SUBTRACTING THESE LEAVES 3866

	1	2	4	8	16	32	64	128	256	512	1024	2048
C4	0	0	0	0	0	0	0	0	0	0	0	0
C4	0	1	1	0	0	1	1	1	0	0	0	0
D4	0	1	1	1	1	1	0	1	1	0	0	0
D4	0	0	1	1	0	1	0	1	0	1	0	0
E4	0	1	1	1	0	0	1	0	1	1	0	0
F4	0	0	1	0	0	0	0	0	0	0	1	0
F4	0	0	0	0	1	1	0	1	0	0	1	0
G4	0	1	0	0	1	0	1	0	1	0	1	0
G4	0	0	1	1	0	1	1	1	1	0	1	0
A4	0	0	1	1	1	1	1	0	0	1	1	0
A4	0	1	1	0	0	0	0	0	1	1	1	0
B4	0	1	1	0	0	0	0	1	1	1	1	0

12-NOTE, 5-OCTAVE STYLUS-OPERATED ORGAN

The circuit shown in Figs. 6-6 and 6-7 could be adapted to a synthesizer or used for a novelty toy to keep the kids occupied (you hope) while you work with your synthesizer (if you can get at it).

Q1 is a multivibrator circuit. The main oscillator consists of Q3, Q4 in Fig. 6-7. The frequency control network is in Fig. 6-8.

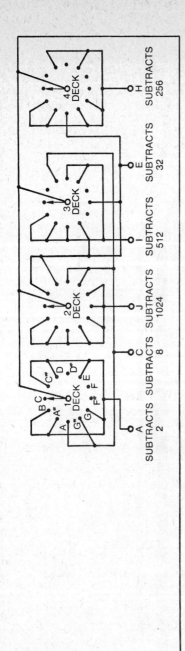
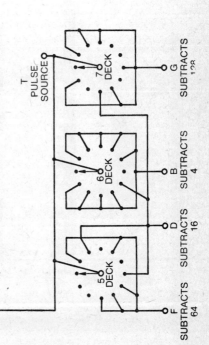

Fig. 6-5. Switch for electronic piano.

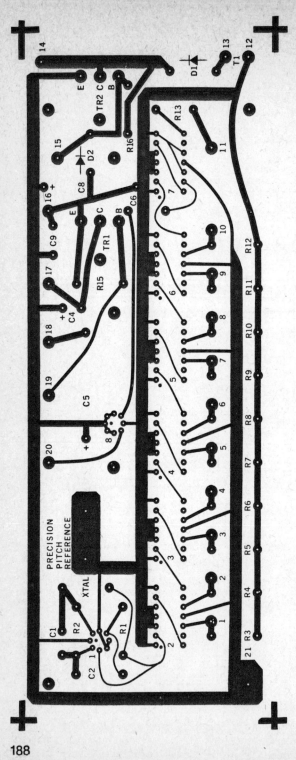

Fig. 6-6. Full-size board layout.

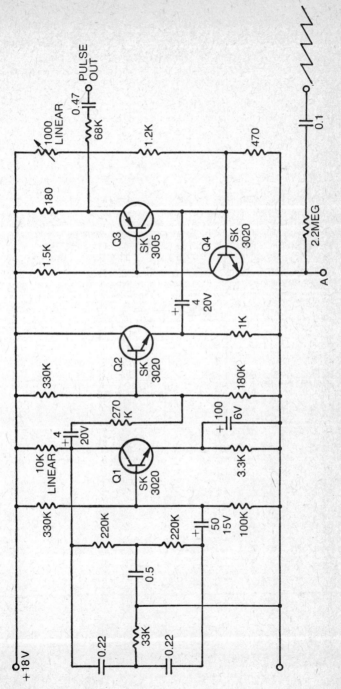

Fig. 6-7. Stylus-operated organ circuit.

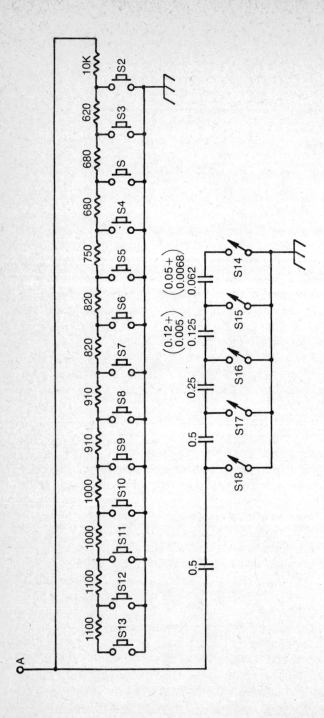

Fig. 6-8. Frequency control network.

7 | Sequencers

Perhaps one of the most neglected areas in electronic music is the sequencer. There are a number of reasons for this. First, very little has been available to the electronic technician and engineer on the subject of electronic music circuits. Organ manufacturers are reluctant to part with circuit information and synthesizer manufacturers seem to be even less anxious.

Naturally, part of this reluctance is based not so much on the hazards of releasing proprietary information as on the concept of a "blind market." If those buying a piece of equipment know nothing about what it contains and have no way of learning its relative merits, then the manufacturer can charge whatever the market will bear and no one will ever question the contents of the equipment in terms of expertise or material cost!

As a direct result, people who could contribute to improved operation, better and less costly manufacturing techniques, and the like never have the information available to start with. In addition, manufacturers tend to go off on their own without regard to standards or what the rest of the industry is doing.

One purpose of this book is to begin to put electronics people in the picture a bit. No standards have been set, but certain principles are certainly evolving. The trend in electronic organs is to have certain programed material, including tempo and chords or accompaniment. There is also a trend toward the types of synthesizer functions that have been included in this book.

Also, music synthesis had a certain "space" quality about it that, though interesting, left a lot to be desired—until a few very talented and imaginative people got into the act. I was persuaded to buy a recording called *Switched On Bach;* what Walter Carlos has done with what can only be called electronic enhancement of classical music is absolutely beautiful if not downright breathtaking.

Instead of the avant-garde 50-note scale, Walter Carlos has stuck to the good old equally tempered scale and the music comes across with such vigor and emotion that one feels Bach would be delighted with the result.

The idea is a very simple one. With tempo, instrument, and waveshape variations, the possible combinations of music with the equally tempered scale must still be mastered by the majority of the world population. If a composer or musician can develop the necessary skill to do what Walter Carlos has done, then why step out and try to prove how smart you are and how stupid the rest of the world is by developing a completely new music system when the one we have has only been touched on?

The message is really directed to the manufacturers and developers of organs and synthesizers. Let's stick to a framework that exists; rather than trying to develop a framework to fit the new flexibility afforded by electronics, let's try to improve on the existing one.

We now have the ability to do some fabulous things in the area of electronic music; one of the biggest assists would be in the area of sequencers that allow the musician to build on an already established theme. The organ manufacturers *are* getting around to it, but the next step should be a programmable machine that would allow a complete melody and accompaniment line to be stored and then used to build on.

The devices that follow do not necessarily point the way but they do suggest some possibilities in first random and then programed sequencing. Each has a tempo generator built in, and although the first argument may be that this detracts from the composer's control of the tempo, let me say that each one could have a foot pedal that would allow for fine or coarse variation in tempo so that argument goes out the window immediately.

RANDOM-TUNE SEQUENCER

The first unit starts with a *tempo oscillator* (see block diagram, Fig. 7-1). The *tempo* could be controlled by a foot pedal. It could be either a potentiometer or a cadmium-sulfide cell with a wedge-type slit to vary the amount of light and thus the resistance.

The rest of the circuitry will have some similarity to the equipment already shown. The result will be a VCO with filter

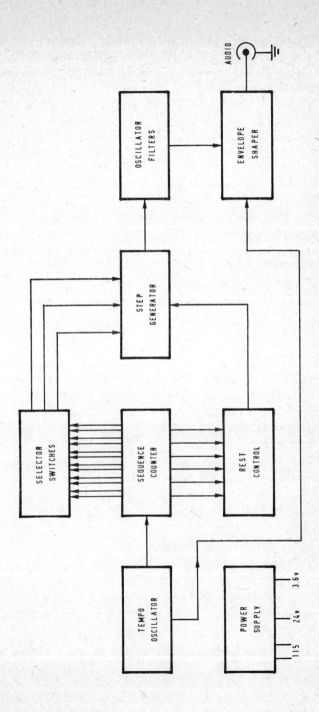

Fig. 7-1. Random-tune generator block diagram.

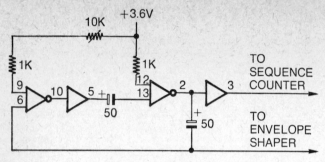

Fig. 7-2. Tempo oscillator.

voicing driven by a random voltage generator and with several keying and triggering facilities. The circuitry could be used with other synthesizer modules, particularly the envelope shaper and the random-control-voltage generator.

Figure 7-2 is the circuit for the tempo oscillator. A Motorola MC799P integrated circuit is used; the circuit drives the envelope shaper to insure synchronous operation and also drives the up/down counter, whose sequence can be reversed.

The counter circuit is shown in Fig. 7-3. The tempo oscillator drives all clock inputs to the 6 flip-flops simultaneously. The sequences generated can be changed using either the up/down switch or the forward/reverse switch. This makes a total of four possible sequences. The counter can be stopped using the play/stop switch. One sequence is shown in Fig. 7-4.

The outputs of this counter are supplied to the random selector switches (Fig. 7-5). Each of these switches can be set to pick up one of the flip-flop outputs, thus further contributing to the number of possible combinations. The flip-flops also feed a rest generator (Fig. 7-6), which can stop the VCO at various points (depending on the setting of the input switches of the rest generator).

The output of the random selector switches of Fig. 7-6 is fed to a summing network in the voltage-controlled oscillator. The voltage-controlled oscillator uses a unijunction transistor as a relaxation oscillator. The NPN transistor from the emitter of the unijunction transistor (2N5129) is used with the rest generator to cut the oscillator off at random times, simulating a rest in music.

The pitch can be controlled by either the pitch control or the inputs to the summing network modified by the 100K controls in the collector circuit of each transistor. The result is

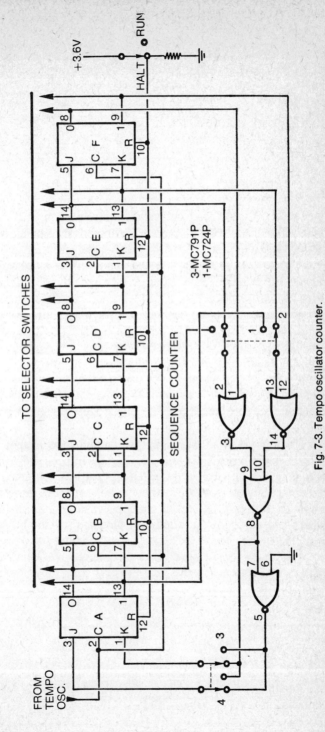

Fig. 7-3. Tempo oscillator counter.

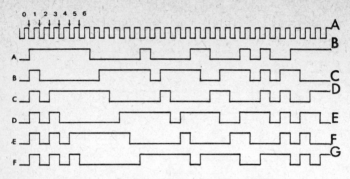

Fig. 7-4. Sequence counter timing diagram;

the ability to control frequency manually as well as by a combination of potentiometers and the sequence being run in the counter.

The single output goes to the voicing filter. The voicing filters can be selected alone or in combination to produce a wider range of sounds.

The output of the voicing filter is fed to the envelope shaper input (Fig. 7-7). The envelope shaper is quite standard from the standpoint of the circuit developing the envelope. It has the usual *sustain, attack*, and *decay* adjustments. What makes the circuit unique is the use of an enhancement-mode MOSFET as a variable attenuator controlled by the output of the envelope shaping circuitry. (The power supply is shown in Fig. 7-8.)

The result is a very high-quality envelope shaper that could be put to use in other circuits besides the one shown here. With all of these circuits hooked up and the switches and controls brought out to a front panel, the variations that can be obtained are almost beyond comprehension. This does not mean that all of the variations are pleasant, it simply means that even this small box can provide hours or years of entertainment for young and old alike without ever running out of possibilities. And you don't have to play it...it plays itself.

PROGRAMED-SEQUENCE RHYTHM GENERATOR

Every rhythm generator available has a selection of foxtrot, waltz, cha-cha, rhumba, and so forth selected by a switch. There is no way to put in an extra drum beat or a cymbal crash in these rhythms. They are fixed.

In working with sequencer ideas, the simplicity of the percussion generators (needing only a pulse to set them into a

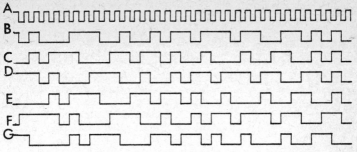

clock pulse train is shown at top.

complete cycle) seemed to make them a natural for a system that would allow the storage and changing of rhythm patterns. The programed-sequence rhythm generator was the result.

Because of the difficulty involved in building low-frequency multivibrators that were also stable, a high frequency of from 2 to 250 Hz was chosen for the tempo generator (Fig. 7-9). The output of this oscillator is divided by 4 to get the tempo range for most music.

This output is applied to a 4-bit counter which has 16 possible states. The counter can also be driven by a manually controlled step generator that allows the program to be placed in the SN7489 storage chips. The output of the 4-bit counter is used to address the locations in the storage cells which can then be set to either binary 0 or 1. The 0 means an instrument will *not* sound, and the 1 means that it *will* sound.

The output of the storage or memory system is applied to gates which trigger the percussion generators. The output of the counter is also fed through a series of gates which allow different sequences to be developed to give $^4/_4$ time, $^3/_4$ time, $^6/_8$ time, and $^9/_8$ time. This covers the majority of possibilities.

With $^4/_4$ time it is possible to program every $^1/_{16}$ note; with $^3/_4$ time, every $^1/_{12}$ note, and with $^6/_8$ time, every $^1/_{12}$ note. In $^9/_8$ time, every $^1/_9$ note can be programed. This simply means that the counter in $^4/_4$ time goes into 16 different states that allow 16 groups of 8 memory locations to be addressed. Thus, in group 1, the drum and blocks may be sounded, in group 2 the bongos and so forth, for a total of 16 different groups of 1 to 8 different instruments in each position.

An SN7447 decoder/divider is used to drive a 7-segment display and a single lamp. The 7-segment display shows 0, 1, 2, 3, 4, 5, 6, or 7 (a total of 8 numerals), indicating which

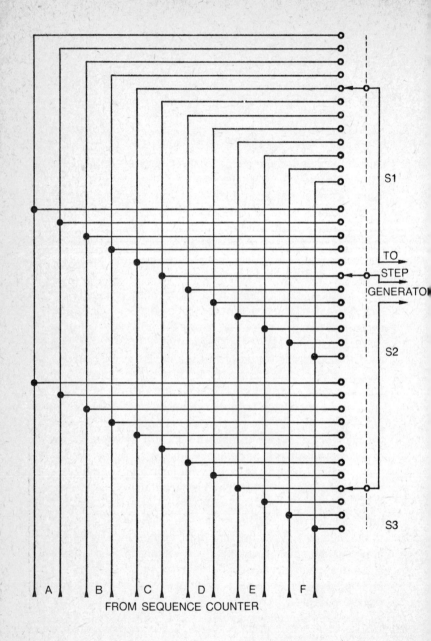

Fig. 7-5. Tempo oscillator selector switches.

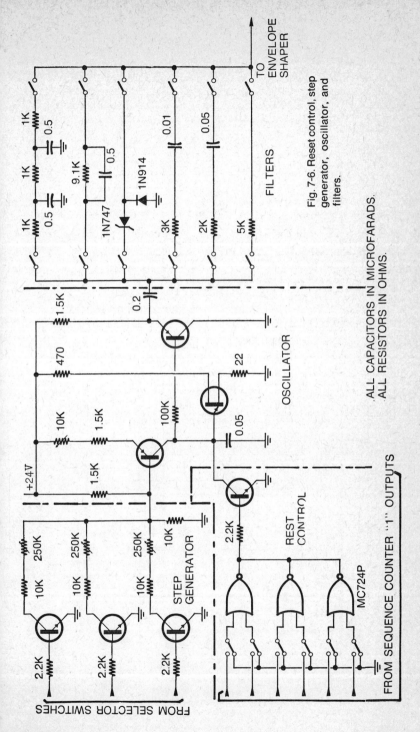

Fig. 7-6. Reset control, step generator, oscillator, and filters.

ALL CAPACITORS IN MICROFARADS.
ALL RESISTORS IN OHMS.

199

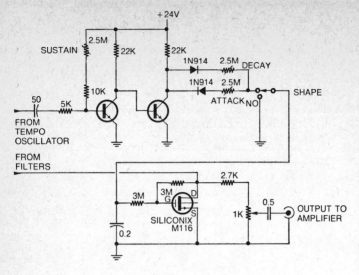

Fig. 7-7. Envelope shaper.

particular part of a measure the sequence is in. The extra lamp shown later in the circuitry is used to indicate the first or second group of 8 possibilities.

The percussion generators that can be used with this device were discussed in prior sections. Figure 7-10 is a block diagram of the rest of the equipment. The tempo generator circuitry is shown in Fig. 7-11. The counter, divider, and reset circuitry is shown in Fig. 7-12, and the memory circuitry and gating is shown in Fig. 7-13.

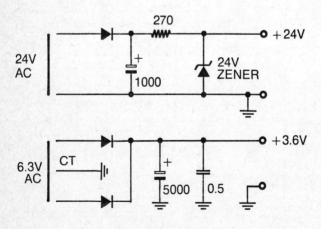

Fig. 7-8. Tempo oscillator power supply.

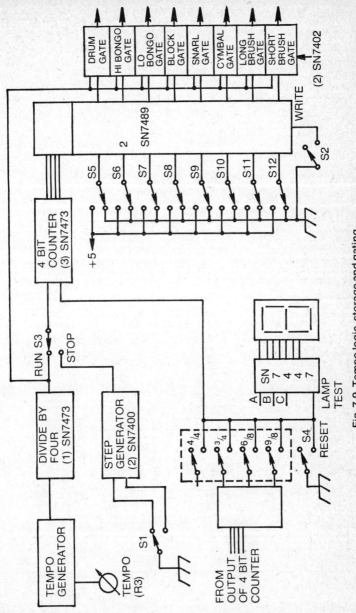

Fig. 7-9. Tempo logic, storage and gating.

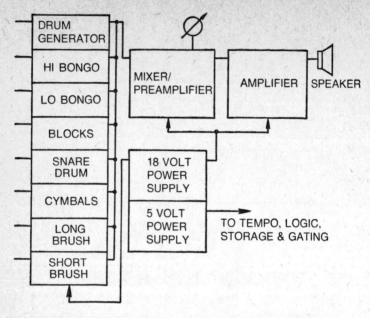

Fig. 7-10. Percussion generators, mixer, and amplifier.

Programing is quite simple. After switching on the power, set S3 to RUN, put all switches (S5 to S12) in the down or 0 position. (These are the switches that store the *sound* or *don't sound* information for the particular rhythm.) Now pressing the WRITE pushbutton (S2) will write all zeros into the memory

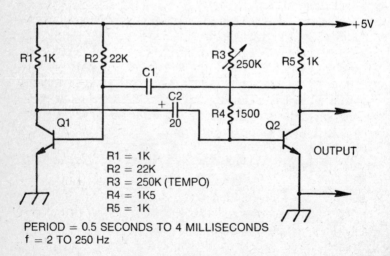

R1 = 1K
R2 = 22K
R3 = 250K (TEMPO)
R4 = 1K5
R5 = 1K

PERIOD = 0.5 SECONDS TO 4 MILLISECONDS
f = 2 TO 250 Hz

Fig. 7-11. Astable multivibrator.

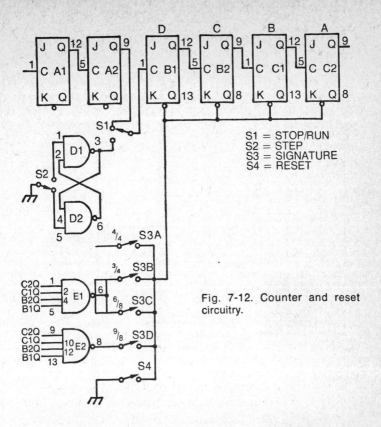

Fig. 7-12. Counter and reset circuitry.

and no instruments will sound. This is equivalent to clearing a computer.

Now put switch S3 in STEP position and push the reset button (Fig. 7-12, S4). The result should be that the small lamp goes out and the 7-segment indicator goes to 0. The program can now be entered. Refer to the Tables 7-1 and 7-2. These show various rhythm combinations found in fixed program rhythm generators. Take the cha-cha in Table 7-2. The tempo is $^4/_4$. To write instruments or an instrument, after the first step, push the STEP button, set up the instrument switches, and then push WRITE.

After resetting, while the indicator is 0, set switch S5 to the up position. This will put a 1 in this first line to sound the drum. Also, the note at the bottom says "short brush every beat," so put S12 up to record a pulse for short brush. This done, press the WRITE button. Now press STEP; the indicator should say 1. Reset the drum and select the long brush. Press WRITE. Press STEP. Select the *hi bongo* and *short brush* with the other

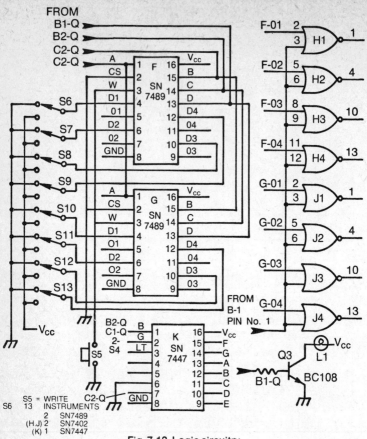

Fig. 7-13. Logic circuitry.

S5 = WRITE
S6 13 INSTRUMENTS
          2   SN7489
(H,J) 2   SN7402
(K) 1   SN7447

¾	WALTZ	V. WALTZ	JAZZ WALTZ
D1			CYMBAL
D2	CYMBAL	CYMBAL	CYMBAL
D4	CYMBAL	CYMBAL	
D5	DRUM	DRUM	DRUM
D6		CYMBAL	CYMBAL
D8			

Table 7-1. Rhythm Generator Sequences.

⁴⁄₄	MARCH/ POLKA	FOX TROT	SAMBA	BOSSA NOVA	WATUSI	CHA CHA	RHUMBA	TANGO
D3	DRUM	DRUM	DRUM	DRUM	DRUM	DRUM	DRUM	DRUM
D4				CONGA			CLAVE	
D5	CYMBAL	CYMBAL	CYMBAL	CONGA	CYMBAL			
D6		CYMBAL	DRUM	DRUM	DRUM	CYMBAL	CLAVE	CYMBAL
D7	DRUM	DRUM	DRUM	DRUM	DRUM	DRUM	DRUM	DRUM
D8				CONGA			CLAVE	
D1	CYMBAL	CYMBAL	CYMBAL	CONGA	CONGA	CONGA	DRUM	DRUM
D2		CYMBAL	CYMBAL	CONGA	CONGA	CONGA	CLAVE	CYMBAL

Table 7-2. Broad-Scale Rhythm Sequences.

SET 1

Code	WALTZ	CHA-CHA	TANGO	ROCK N' ROLL	BEGUINE	SAMBA	MAMBO	FOX TROT	RHUMBA	BOSSA NOVA	QUICK STEP	WESTERN	No.
B101	DRUM L. BRUSH	DRUM	DRUM	DRUM	DRUM	DRUM	DRUM HI BONGO	DRUM	DRUM	DRUM HI BONGO	LONG BRUSH SH BRUSH	DRUM	0
B201	✕	LONG BRUSH			LONG BRUSH	LO BONGO		LONG BRUSH SH BRUSH	HI BONGO			✕	1
B301	✕	HI BONGO	HI BONGO	HI BONGO	LO BONGO	LO BONGO	HI BONGO		LONG BRUSH	HI BONGO	SH BRUSH		
B401						DRUM LONG BRUSH	LO BONGO LONG BRUSH		LO BONGO			LO BONGO	2
B102	SH BRUSH	HI BONGO	HI BONGO	DRUM	LO BONGO	DRUM	HI BONGO	DRUM	LO BONGO	HI BONGO	SH BRUSH		3
B202	✕	HI BONGO		HI BONGO	HI BONGO				HI BONGO			✕	4
B302	✕	HI BONGO	HI BONGO	HI BONGO	LO BONGO	HI BONGO	HI BONGO	SH BRUSH	HI BONGO	HI BONGO	SH BRUSH	LO BONGO	5
B402			HI BONGO LONGBRUSH	HI BONGO			LO BONGO		LO BONGO				

SET 2

Code	WALTZ	CHA-CHA	TANGO	ROCK N' ROLL	BEGUINE	SAMBA	MAMBO	FOX TROT	RHUMBA	BOSSA NOVA	QUICK STEP	WESTERN	No.
B101	DRUM L. BRUSH	DRUM	DRUM	DRUM	DRUM	DRUM	DRUM HI BONGO	DRUM	DRUM	DRUM	LONG BRUSH SH BRUSH	DRUM	6
B201	✕	LONG BRUSH	LO BONGO	HI BONGO	LONG BRUSH	LO BONGO	LO BONGO	LONG BRUSH SH BRUSH	LONG BRUSH	HI BONGO		✕	7
B301	✕	HI BONGO	LO BONGO	HI BONGO	HI BONGO	DRUM LONG BRUSH	HI BONGO	DRUM			SH BRUSH	HI BONGO	0
B401				DRUM		DRUM	LO BONGO LONG BRUSH					HI BONGO	1
B102	SH BRUSH	LO BONGO	LO BONGO	HI BONGO	LO BONGO	HI BONGO	HI BONGO	DRUM		HI BONGO	SH BRUSH		
B202	SH BRUSH LO BONGO	LO BONGO	LO BONGO		LO BONGO		HI BONGO	SH BRUSH					2
B302	✕	HI BONGO	LO BONGO LONG BRUSH	HI BONGO			LO BONGO	SH BRUSH			SH BRUSH	✕	3
B402	SHORT BRUSH EVERY BEAT	SHORT BRUSH EVERY BEAT	SHORT BRUSH EVERY BEAT	SHORT BRUSH EVERY BEAT	SHORT BRUSH EVERY BEAT	SHORT BRUSH EVERY BEAT	SHORT BRUSH EVERY BEAT	SHORT BRUSH EVERY BEAT	SHORT BRUSH EVERY BEAT	SHORT BRUSH EVERY BEAT	SHORT BRUSH EVERY BEAT	SHORT BRUSH EVERY BEAT	

switches reset, and press WRITE. Continue this procedure to the end of the column.

When the last instrument is recorded, place all instrument selection switches in the 0 position and switch the STEP/RUN switch to RUN. You will hear the rhythm you recorded being played over and over exactly as the preprogramed rhythm generators do it.

The resulting rhythm can be altered and improved or changed in any way you like simply by re-recording the sections you want to change.

The recording procedure is also much faster than it sounds when it is being explained. The thing is that using the modern 1024-, 2048-, and 4096-bit MOS memory chips, complete sequences of music could be played just as this rhythm generator is played. The key strokes could be encoded to cut down the number of memory chips required and instead of a player piano, you'd have a player organ with synthesizer capabilities!

Appendix
The 2720
Synthesizer Keyboard

Regardless of the synthesizer you build, during the calibration procedure you will be working with a VCO that has been roughly calibrated following the tuning procedure outlined in that section. The purpose of that procedure was to make the input voltage/output frequency response conform as closely as possible to the graph shown in Fig. A1. While the slope of this line is not particularly critical (small variations can be compensated for at the keyboard), the fact that it intersects the origin (zero frequency for zero control voltage) is of critical importance.

To clarify this, assume for a moment that when the oscillator was calibrated, errors in the VOM caused the actual response of the VCO to be as shown in Fig. A2. This graph is exaggerated but it is typical of the errors that occur in actual practice. Performing the first part of the calibration procedure that will follow would set up the three-octave interval from C5 to C2. Everything is fine *at this point*; it really doesn't matter that the low end of the keyboard is about 0.45V rather than the design value of 0.625V, because the trimmers on the voltage divider can make up the difference.

Now the problem: When we try to drop the keyboard an octave by pushing the C5 key and cranking back the pitch knob

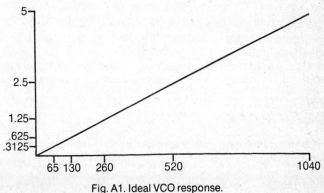

Fig. A1. Ideal VCO response.

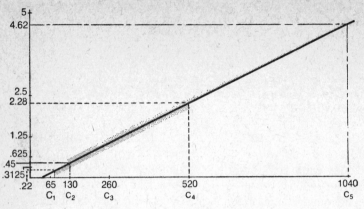

Fig. A2. Practical VCO response.

until we hear C4, we discover that the rest of the keyboard is no longer in tune. The reason is that turning the pitch knob has the effect of dividing the voltage at each tap on the divider by a constant factor (0.493 in this case); but when the voltage at the low end of the keyboard is divided by this term the result is 0.22V corresponding to a note considerably higher than the intended C1.

A part of the keyboard calibration procedure will be concerned with calibrating the response curve of the VCO so that it does, in fact, intersect the origin. Two methods of calibrating the keyboard will be outlined. The first method uses an oscilloscope and signal generator, while the second relies on a tuned musical instrument as a pitch reference. This reference could also be one of the pitch references described elsewhere. The purposes of both these procedures will be the same: first, to exactly calibrate the voltage drop from one end of the keyboard to the other and, second, to set the proper voltage intervals using the trimmer potentiometers. Neither method has an appreciable edge as far as accuracy or simplicity of procedure is concerned.

The procedure given here is written for the keyboard shown in Fig. A3. This keyboard is part of the PAIA 2720 synthesizer kit, and is designed to mate with the circuitry described in Chapter 5.

CALIBRATION PROCEDURE

Connect the VCO to the power supply but do not install it permanently at this point. It may be necessary to make some additional adjustments to it.

Fig. A3. Complete 2720A synthesizer.

Method 1, Using Test Equipment

As shown in Fig. A4, arrange the VCO, an audio generator, and the oscilloscope so that the scope will display a Lissajous pattern such as the ones shown in Fig. A5. Set the frequency of the audio generator to 260 Hz and apply a control voltage to the VCO so that a pattern appears on the scope. Adjust the vertical gain of the scope and the output of the audio source so that the pattern fills the screen. Allow the VCO to run for about 10 minutes so that temperatures can stabilize.

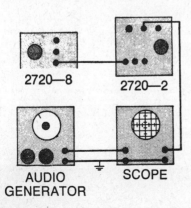

2720—8   2720—2

AUDIO GENERATOR   SCOPE

Fig. A4. Synthesizer keyboard test setup.

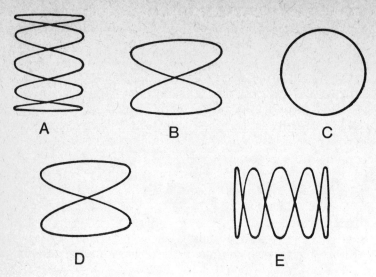

Fig. A5. Lissajous patterns for keyboard calibration.

Before starting the calibration procedure, set all trimmer potentiometers on the keyboard voltage divider circuit board to the midpoint of their rotation.

1) Remove the external control voltage source from the VCO and set the low end trimmer (R21, located at the rear of the case) to about the midpoint of its rotation.

2) Press and hold the highest key of the keyboard (C) and adjust the *pitch* knob (R20, located on the keyboard control panel) for the pattern shown in Fig. A5-E, indicating that the output of the VCO is exactly four times the reference frequency. The test oscillator need not be exactly 260 Hz; the oscillator should be reasonably stable because the frequency is not changed—the patterns are used to set the VCO to exact multiples of that reference frequency.

3) Press the lowest C key on the keyboard (first key) and adjust low-end trimmer R21 for the Lissajous pattern shown in Fig. A5-B, indicating that the VCO is exactly half of the reference frequency.

4) Once again press the highest C and check to see if the frequency has changed slightly (it probably has). Readjust the *pitch* knob for the pattern shown in Fig. A5-E.

5) Go back and forth between the highest and lowest C until the patterns corresponding to these keys are stable without further adjustment. A slight rotation of the traces is acceptable as long as they can be recognized.

6) Press and hold the highest C key while rotating the *pitch* knob counterclockwise until the point is reached at which the scope displays the pattern shown in Fig. A5-D, indicating that the frequency of the VCO is exactly twice that of the reference.

7) Press and hold the lowest C key and observe the scope trace. It should look like Fig. A5-A, indicating that the VCO is running at ¼ the frequency of the reference.

Proceed with setting the intervals, starting with step 8. If the trace is not as shown in Fig. A5-A (and chances are it won't be), adjust the *zero* control of the VCO (R4) until you get this trace. Repeat steps 1 through 7 until the patterns displayed in each step are stable (or have only a *slow* rotation) without further adjustment of the keyboard low-end trimmer or the VCO *zero* trimmer.

8) Once again press and hold the highest key and rotate the *pitch* knob clockwise until the pattern shown in Fig. A5-E is obtained.

9) The trimmers for the intermediate C's of the keyboard are marked with arrowheads on the voltage-divider circuit board. Press and hold the key corresponding to the higher of these two intermediate C's and adjust its trimmer until the pattern shown in Fig. A5-D is obtained.

10) Similarly, press and hold the key corresponding to the lower of the two intermediate C's and adjust its trimmer for a stable trace like the one shown in Fig. A5-C. If a change of more than 45° of the rotation of the trimmers in steps 9 and 10 is needed to produce the required patterns, it may indicate a solder bridge, cold solder joint, or improper resistor placement on the voltage-divider circuit board.

11) Lower the keyboard an octave and check the traces of the intermediate C's against Fig. A5-B and A5-C. It is possible that there will be slight nonlinearities in the response of the VCO that cause the intermediate C's to differ slightly as the *pitch* control is changed. For either of these C's it may be necessary to split the difference for optimum performance. Remember that you are seeing very small changes in frequency when using Lissajous patterns. In Fig. A5-B, for example, a complete rotation of the pattern every second corresponds to 0.5 Hz difference between the VCO and reference frequencies.

The major intervals of the keyboard are now set and you have gone as far as you can using commonly available test equipment. At this point you can either set the semitone intervals by ear or by comparison with a tuned musical instrument. Don't scoff at the "by ear" method. Most people can come amazingly close once they have the octave intervals set. If you can't *hear* the difference, it doesn't matter a lot anyway. Adjust the pitch of each note by setting the corresponding trimmer potentiometer on the keyboard voltage-divider circuit board. Do not adjust the C trimmers.

Method 2, Using a Tuned Musical Reference

Connect the *pulse* output of the VCO to the line level input of a hi-fi or instrument amplifier and temporarily jumper a constant control voltage (from one of the power supply bias sources) to one of the control voltage inputs. Allow the VCO to run for about 10 minutes to allow temperatures to stabilize. Jumper the OUT jack from the keyboard control panel to the left-hand control voltage input jack and center all trimmers on the voltage divider circuit board as well as the pitch and low-end trimmer potentiometer.

1) Press and hold the highest C on the keyboard and adjust the pitch knob for zero beat between this note and the second C above middle C on the reference instrument.

2) Press and hold the lowest C on the keyboard and adjust for zero beat between this note and the C below middle C on the reference instrument.

3) Go back and forth between steps 1 and 2 until there is a zero beat for both notes without further adjustment.

4) While holding down the highest C on the keyboard, turn the *pitch* control counterclockwise until the note produced is zero beat with the C above middle C of the reference instrument.

5) Check the lowest C on the keyboard. If it is zero beat with the second C below middle C of the reference instrument, you can proceed to step 6. If the two notes are not the same, zero beat them by adjusting the *zero* control of the VCO. Repeat steps 1 through 5 until all notes are identical without any adjustment of either the VCO *zero* trimmer or the keyboard low-end trimmer.

6) Once the high- and low-end adjustments are made on the keyboard and VCO, the two intermediate C's may be set using the pitch control to return the highest C to zero beat with the second C above middle C, then using the designated trimmers on the voltage-divider circuit board to zero beat the second and third C down the keyboard with the C above middle C, and middle C, respectively.

7) Press each key in turn and adjust the corresponding trimmer potentiometer for zero beat with the corresponding note on the tuned reference instrument.

USING THE 2720-8 KEYBOARD

The purpose of any controller is to provide a manually variable source of voltage which can be used to change the parameters of a VCO or other system.

If the controller is to be a type of keyboard, there are some additional design objectives that must be added to simplify generating a voltage. For instance, for maximum versatility there should be some way to signal the rest of the modules when a key is pressed and when it is released. The PAIA 2720-8 provides these features by supplying two types of trigger output function.

The first trigger output is a voltage step that goes high when any key is pressed and stays high until all keys are released. This trigger could be used directly as a control voltage, but it will most often be used to start the 2720-4 function generator. Using this trigger will cause the output of the function generator to remain high as long as any key is held down.

The second trigger output is a short-duration voltage pulse that rises whenever any key is pressed. All keys must be released before another pulse can be generated. This trigger output will always be used as an initiating pulse to the function generator.

Many of the effects produced using the 2720 will use the end of the voltage step trigger output as a signal to begin processing the decay portion of the sound. Since the step does not end until the keys are released, there must be some way to hold the voltage that last appeared at the output of the controller; otherwise, when the key is released the controller output will drop to zero, causing the VCO (or other module connected to the controller output) to go to its zero control voltage condition (no output in the case of the VCO).

The sample-and-hold circuit that is part of the controller package solves this problem by serving as a short-term analog memory. Every time a key is pressed the circuit stores the voltage corresponding to that key for a period of time greater than 20 seconds or until the next key is pressed. No apologies need be made for the sample-and-hold. It is one of the best designs available; and 20 seconds is more than enough for most applications.

The design of the controller provides for three octaves of selectable control voltage, but since the range of the VCO is considerably greater than three octaves, provision has been made for raising or lowering the keyboard a full octave, thereby giving it a four-octave capability. The pitch knob can also be set to any position between the extremes of its rotation without altering the chromatic tuning of the keyboard. Manual glissando or very slow tremolo can be added to a note simply by holding down the key and rotating the *pitch* knob.

Pressing two keys simultaneously will not produce the notes corresponding to both keys (since only one control voltage can be generated at any one time) but it will produce a tone somewhere between the notes. Many interesting nonchromatic melody lines can be produced by pressing two keys at the same time.

OPERATION OF THE CONTROLS

Pressing any key causes a preset voltage to appear at the control voltage output jack. In most cases these voltages will be set to generate a chromatic scale, but other tunings are possible.

The *pitch* knob on the control panel allows the entire keyboard to be lowered an octave from the standard tuning. Counterclockwise rotation of the knob decreases output voltage for any given key.

The uppermost pin jack on the control panel provides access to a voltage that changes from 0 to $+5V$ when any key is pressed. This voltage remains at the high level as long as the key is held down.

The middle pin jack provides access to a short-duration trigger pulse that is generated when any key is pressed. All keys must be released for the pulse generator to reset before it can produce another pulse. Reset time is on the order 0.1 msec.

DESIGN ANALYSIS

Reduced to basics, the controller is nothing more than a switch controllable voltage divider but it starts to get a little more complicated as housekeeping functions are added. In addition to the voltage divider, the circuit includes both the current source, trigger circuit, and sample-and-hold circuitry.

The constant-current source is a standard design built around Q1 and using the voltage drop across the series combination of D1 and D2 as a reference. The output of the current source is regulated by changing the DC feedback with emitter resistor R20. The current source feeds the voltage divider shown in Fig. A6 and represented by R_K.

The voltage divider is implemented with a string of fixed and variable resistors, as shown. In order that the voltage output of the string be exponential, to duplicate the exponential nature of the equally tempered musical scale, the resistance values are calculated and selected so that the resistance of any parallel pair in the string is approximately 1.059 times greater than the resistance of the pair directly below it. In order to compensate for tolerance pileups over the length of the voltage divider, the trimmers for the octave points corresponding to the two middle C's of the keyboard are arranged so that they can raise and lower the voltage at those points over a 6- to 8-semitone spread rather than through a single semitone as are the other trimmers.

There are two sets of contacts associated with each key. The first set of contacts switches a voltage from the voltage divider corresponding to the key pressed, and applies it to point E in Fig. A6. The second set of contacts are common to all keys and close whenever any key is pressed. This set of contacts causes the sample-and-hold circuit to store a new sample and also provides the step and pulse trigger outputs.

When any key is pressed it first causes the voltage pickoff switch to close, thereby applying a voltage corresponding to the position of the key to be applied to C1. C1 is an integrating capacitor to bypass any noise that might be generated by dirt on the contacts. Next, the switch common to all keys closes. A current begins to flow through R11, R15, and R16. The current flow through R16 causes a voltage drop to appear across this resistor; this voltage is applied to J3, where it serves as the step output. The step is differentiated by C5 and appears at J2 as the pulse output. Diode D6 serves to shunt to ground the negative pulse that would appear when the step returns to zero.

The current flow through R11 causes a voltage drop that allows current flow through R12 to turn on Q4. With Q4 on, current can flow through R13, R14, D4, and D5 to ground. This current flow raises the junction of R13 and R14 to a voltage that is high enough to insure that field effect transistor Q2 will be turned on. The voltage that appears across the series string of R15 and R16 causes C4 to charge through the forward-biased D5.

The sample-and-hold circuit can further be broken down into a comparator (IC), a high-impedance FET source follower (Q3), and a switch (Q2). The comparator is constantly

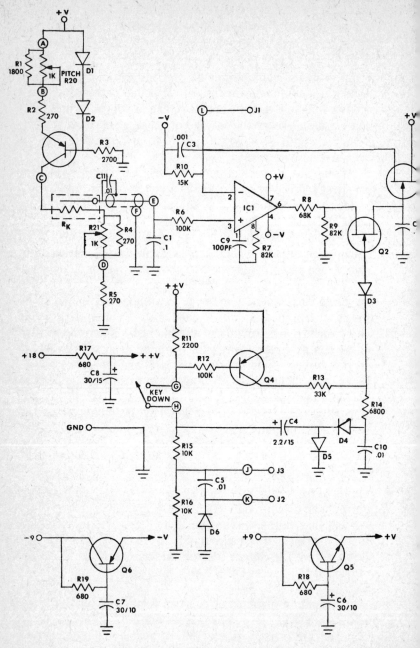

Fig. A6. Keyboard control schematic.

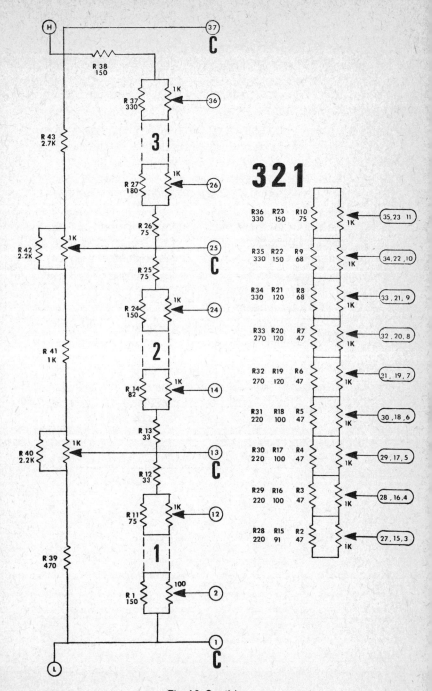

Fig. A6. Cont'd.

217

comparing the input from the keyboard to the output appearing across the load resistor of source follower R10. The state of this comparator has no effect on holding capacitor C2 (and consequently the output of the source follower for which this capacitor is an input) until switch Q2 is turned on. With Q2 on, the comparator works to make the voltage at its " + " and " − " inputs identical. When the voltages are identical, the circuit is in a balanced condition.

When the key is released, Q4 turns off, which removes the current flow through D4 and D5. Simultaneously, the positive side of C4 is allowed to go to ground through R15 and R16. In this configuration the negative side of C4 is connected to C10 through D4 and D4 is forward-biased under these conditions. The charge that was on C4 now dumps onto C10; and since the positive side of C4 is at ground, the ungrounded end of C10 is pushed about −15V with respect to ground. This high negative voltage is applied to the gate of Q2, thereby turning the FET off. All possible leakage paths for the voltage across C10 are, at this point, either reverse-biased diodes, *off* transistors, or the reverse-biased gate junction of Q2. Since there is no discharge path for C10, its voltage remains high and holds Q2 off for an extended period of time.

With Q2 off, holding capacitor C2 is isolated from any discharge path, but the voltage across this capacitor still serves as the input for the source follower; so the output voltage at point L does not change. Q5 and Q6 serve as capacitance multipliers for filter capacitors C6 and C7.

Index

Index